Refined
BY
CHRIST

OTHER BOOKS AND AUDIO BOOKS
BY TONI SORENSON:

Master

Messiah

Defined by Christ

Women of Christ: Of Infinite Worth

Redemption Road

The Shaken Earth

Behold Your Little Ones

I Will Go, I Will Do

Heroes of the Book of Mormon

Heroes of the Bible

Where Can I Turn for Peace?

He Knows Your Heart: Inspiring Thoughts for Women

*Of These Emblems: Coming Closer to Christ
through the Sacrament*

Refined BY CHRIST

*Seeking His Image
in Our Countenance*

TONI SORENSON

Covenant Communications, Inc.

Cover image: *In the World, Not of the World* © Greg Olsen. For more information, go to www. gregolsen.com

Cover design © 2013 by Covenant Communications, Inc.

Published by Covenant Communications, Inc.
American Fork, Utah

Printed in Canada
First Printing: March 2013

20 19 18 17 16 15 14 13   10 9 8 7 6 5 4 3 2 1

ISBN 978-1-62108-171-5

REFINE:
To free from impurities, from moral imperfection;
to improve by pruning or polishing;
to free from what is coarse, vulgar, or uncouth;
to become pure or perfected

And he shall sit [as] a refiner and purifier
—Mal. 3:3; also D&C 128:24

For my friend Cindy A.,
who wherever she goes
brings three things:
help,
hope,
and happiness

CONTENTS

INTRODUCTION

NOT SO LONG AGO I was on a very small airplane that encountered some problems on takeoff. I happened to be wedged in the seat directly behind our only pilot, a brave and I'm sure highly skilled Israeli woman. I could tell right away that she was concerned by the way she kept checking the instrument panel, white-knuckling the steering wheel, and whispering rapidly—not in Hebrew, but in Swahili, for we were gliding over the vast flatlands of the Serengeti.

The pilot was a champ. She did nothing to let on to the ten passengers that anything was wrong. They did not have the vantage I had. I could see her hands tremble. I could see sweat bead on her forehead and drip off her nose. I could hear the tremor in her voice and picked up on words like *hatari* (danger), *baya* (bad), and *Inshallah* (if God wills).

I didn't know what was wrong and I'm not sure she did at that point. I figured it must not be so bad because she kept flying until we were within viewing distance of the highest standing mountain in all of Africa, Kilimanjaro. For a time I got lost in the majesty and beauty of the mountain. My daughter had climbed to the top a few years earlier, and my thoughts turned to her and what it must have been like to have accomplished such a feat. I missed my children back at home in the United States and dreamed of a future day when we could all share Africa together.

Our altitude dipped, and the pilot pointed out a herd of elephants; soon we could also see the bold stripes of zebras and the lumbering towers of giraffes. A red light suddenly flashed on the instrument panel, and the pilot's lips start muttering what I took to be a prayer. She was back on the radio speaking rapidly. We were descending slowly enough, but that didn't mean my stomach didn't lurch. Down, down we glided until we were close enough to the ground to see a pride of lions resting beneath a shade tree. That's about the time I thought we might actually crash. That's about the time I started to think of all the things I still wanted to accomplish in my life. I wanted to be a better mother. I wanted to live to see my grandchildren grow. I wanted to lose weight and get healthy. I wanted to travel the rest of the world and write stories that would encourage people's faith in Heavenly Father and Jesus Christ. Mostly, I just wanted to be better than I had been. I too bowed my head and prayed.

I don't remember if the pilot ever told the rest of the passengers, but she did crank around to tell me, "We have lost a tire."

"Is that all?" I asked, relieved.

"We had three. Now we have two."

"Oh." I didn't realize the challenge of landing a plane safely without equal support on both sides. "*Baya?*" I asked.

She nodded and wiped sweat from her brow.

The runway was a long, skinny stretch of red dirt surrounded by nothing except waving African grass that camouflaged both Africa's beauty and savagery.

The pilot was brilliant. I watched her fingers grip the wheel and hold it as steady as she could. What a ride! She landed that plane—not exactly straight, but safe enough.

Everyone cheered and clapped. The pilot turned around and gave me a quick hug and whispered, "*Asante sana.*"

Why was she thanking me?

"I saw you pray, and to pray always helps."

Everyone deplaned and began snapping photos of the flat tire and mangled wheel.

A furnace of African heat blasted me, and I walked down the runway a bit, looking at the grass—it was all I could see in any direction. I knew there were animals out there but I couldn't see them from the ground. I closed my eyes and prayed again. This time it began with gratitude and a plea, "Help me to know what you want me to do."

I heard a gentle, loving admonishment: *Choose life.*

I understood, because the scripture in Deuteronomy 30:19–20 was very familiar to me: "I have set before you life and death, blessing and cursing; therefore choose life, that both you and your descendants may live; that you may love the Lord your God, that you may obey His voice, and that you may cling to Him, for He is your life and the length of your days."

Isn't that what we all want—to live with passion and purpose and progression? I know I do. But sometimes—most times, in my case—life is tough, even cruel and unfair. I am not a woman who wakes the sun up for scripture time, who counts her carbs and never complains. Heavenly Father has been more than generous to me, and I am deeply grateful for my life and my blessings, but I've been through the wringer and it shows. You know what? I wouldn't trade my scars if that meant I had to relearn the lessons they taught me. I don't want to go back. I want to move forward. How to do that—not my way, but the Lord's way—is what this book is all about.

I spent many years believing that mortality was something I had to endure until it was over. Adversity was an enemy that stalked me like a ravenous lion. I felt like I did on that plane: a little afraid and a lot uncertain. My past shadowed me, my feelings of inadequacy overwhelmed me, and guilt was my constant companion. No matter how hard I tried, my efforts were never good enough.

That was no way to live, and I don't live like that anymore. Why? Jesus, in His mercy and infinite patience, taught me nine lessons that changed my perspective, my attitude, and, subsequently, my everything. It started with the scripture in Malachi 3:3 that refers to the Lord as a refiner. *What does that mean?* I wondered, I pondered, I explored. The more I learned, the more enlightened and empowered I became. A single scripture shifted my spiritual life back into balance, and I'm excited to share with you just how that can happen for you also.

CHAPTER ONE

A Little Better

"Our task is to become our best selves."
—President Thomas S. Monson

I WAS NERVOUS. I'D NEVER been in a leper colony and wasn't sure what the doctor was going to expect me to do. I had scant medical training and was really no more than a willing heart and unskilled hands.

"Take this tub and fill it with water from the tap. Wash the wounds with this bit of soap and then be sure to carry the diseased water far from the colony to dump it. Not even the lepers want the filthy water to seep back into their soil."

I looked down at the wedge of gritty, gray soap that lay in my palm. I had so many questions, but patients were lining up, and I had come to India to do whatever was required of me.

The only water tap in miles and miles was under lock and key. The chief of the colony, a man whose own body was ravaged with leprosy, allowed me to fill my plastic tub. In a mix of Tamil and gestures, he repeated the warning the doctor had given me: "Take the diseased water outside the colony to dump it."

It's hard to find words to describe my emotions (perhaps a mix of honor and horror) as I sat at the feet of my first leper and did my best to clean infection and dirt from the nubs that were once toes. Silently, I prayed like I had never prayed before. Then the man was maneuvered on to the nurse who was waiting to redress his wounds.

Carefully, so that I would not spill a single drop from the plastic tub, I made my way down a narrow, overgrown pathway (careful to watch for snakes). When I was far from the border of the colony, I dumped the foul water and went back to have my tub refilled.

My next patient was an elderly woman who would not meet my gaze. She lifted her leg to show me that leprosy had claimed all of her toes and left her with only a stub of a severely infected foot. I did my best to be gentle as I worked to clean her gaping sores.

Right way the woman seemed agitated. She spoke rapidly in Tamil, but I didn't understand. I thought I was hurting her so I washed more tenderly. She only grew more irritated with me. I smiled. She didn't. Her tone turned severe as I tried my best to tend to her wound with compassion. She writhed this way and that; all the time I was gently washing pus and maggots from the bottom of her foot. Finally, in a frustration I could not fathom, she used her other foot to suddenly kick the tub of water directly at my face. Water, now gray with infection, splashed into my eyes, in my mouth, up my nose, and into my ears.

The angry woman managed to get herself down the line to the waiting nurse.

You can imagine how I felt sitting on the ground, drenched and absolutely confused. No one paid much notice to me except a few people who backed away. I stood up slowly and took my plastic tub, with the few drops that were left in the bottom, and walked down that winding pathway to where it was permissible to empty it.

I wept as I tried to wipe my face and clean myself. The prayer I uttered went something like this: *Heavenly Father, now I understand. I came from the other side of the world to help serve that woman and this is how I get treated. Now I know how Jesus felt when the lepers did not thank Him.*

It was as if I could see my Savior smiling down at me, loving but somewhat amused. Through His Holy Spirit I felt a voice call me away from my pity party to a higher plane: *Toni, you have no idea. Go back to that woman. Kneel before her and kiss and hug her. Tell her how much I love her.*

Go back? I started to protest. *Did you see how she treated me?*

Go, the Spirit repeated.

But she doesn't believe in you. She doesn't even know you.

Go.

I don't know that I've ever felt such an urging to rise above and beyond my selfish self, to do the hard thing, to do what Christ would have done. And so I went back. The nurse was just finishing up with the bandages, and I knelt in front of the woman, who looked at me with what I took to be utter disdain. I kissed her cheek anyway and put my arms around her and whispered in her ear just how much God loved her.

She did not understand me but she completely understood the Spirit of God. It translated my broken Tamil and spoke right to her heart. I could sense it in the return embrace she offered. I could see it in the tears that glided down her weathered cheeks. I could feel it burn in my own heart. It wasn't about me. It wasn't even about the woman. It was about God's love for every one of His children.

It was only later, when all of the patients were attended to, that the Indian nurse explained what I had not known. One of the side effects of leprosy is numbness in the affected areas. The woman had been asking me not to cleanse her wound with gentleness but with vigor. She wanted to feel the sensation of the scrubbing and the sting of the soap so that she could be sure her infection was being expelled. It was no wonder she was agitated with me; she thought my timidity was leaving infection behind to fester and cause her greater suffering.

To Follow Jesus

That single experience turned my heart inside out. It opened my mind to ideas I'd never known and planted a hope in me that I could be—that I *should* be—something more, something better. It made me realize that if we truly follow Jesus Christ, the path is not easy; in fact, it's the most challenging journey possible.

Often we are asked to go back, to give love when love was not extended to us. We are asked to forgive when we are the ones who were wronged. We are asked to do more than our share. We are expected to apologize when we believe *we* should be the one hearing, "I'm sorry." We are required to serve without recognition, to sacrifice until it hurts, to not give up when all we want to do is quit.

You are called to something great because you are capable of greatness. You have the personality, the intellect, the will, and the support to do whatever that "great" feat is. It does not have to be big to be great. When you were born into this world, you came equipped and prepared to accomplish the work assigned only to you, the mission you and you alone can fulfill. As President Gordon B. Hinckley counseled us, "Believe in yourself, my brothers and sisters. You are a child of God. You do have something of divinity within you. Believe in your capacity to do great and good things" ("Inspirational Thoughts," *Ensign*, July 1998, 4).

Tenacity and New Teeth

Elder Bruce R. McConkie's mother, Vivian, was a valiant woman whose dedication to the gospel and to her family is legendary. She was demure and delicate in stature but mighty in spirit. When she was president of her ward Relief Society in Salt Lake City, she made a dental appointment to have all of her teeth pulled. That's thirty-two teeth, considering she still had her wisdom teeth. Imagine what that felt like. The dentist then fit a pair of hard porcelain dentures into her sore, swollen mouth. Vivian McConkie got up out of that dental chair and walked several city blocks at a brisk pace. She had a Relief Society meeting to conduct and wasn't going to let a little thing like new teeth keep her from her commitment (Margaret Vivian McConkie Pope, *Legacy*, a private family history, 2010).

I shudder at the thought of what Vivian McConkie suffered just so she could be on time for Relief Society. I cringe to think how I balked in India because I didn't want to cross a leper colony to hug someone in desperate need of a hug. Instead, I wanted to feel sorry for myself and draw the sympathy of others. A patient, loving Refiner wanted something better for both of us. The woman felt divine love and my heart was changed forever. Christ knows that every decision we make between right and wrong or between better and best matters. "It makes a difference to all eternity whether we do right or wrong today" (James Freeman Clarke, *Elbert Hubbard's Scrap Book* [1923], 95).

I wish I could sit beside you and we could read the pages of this book together. In a way, I suppose that is exactly what we're doing. Please know that this is a labor of love—my love—but more importantly, God's love. It is a call for all of us to look back and realize how far we've come, then to rise up and live higher than we have. It's a guide for doing just that. I believe we are all born for greatness, yet most of us mire in the mediocrity of life. We become complacent—or worse, discouraged and stagnant. We damn ourselves by not progressing. I want us to lunge forward in faith and renewed energy, onward and upward to a life that is pure and powerful, joyful beyond worldly comprehension.

All Satan Has to Do

As Latter-day Saints, our standard is set high. At least it *should* be high, for where much is given, much is required. We have been given the standard set by the Lord for those who take upon them His name and profess to follow Him. We claim modern prophets and continuing revelation. We testify that we have the gift of the Holy Ghost among a myriad of other spiritual gifts.

Much that is required sometimes becomes *too much*. We break. We quit. We label ourselves failures. Guess what? When we do that we're wrong. We need to get back on the horse that bucks us off. Make another dinner and wash the same set of dishes we've washed a zillion times. Listen to a child's prayer over and over. When we fall, we need to rise again.

Satan doesn't want us to know this little truth. He wants us to think that we are how we feel. Take a minute to think deeply about that. How we feel is not who we are. We might feel like failures but as long as we are still trying, we are not failures. We are works in progress. To keep us from remembering this, Satan discourages us. He robs us of hope while he reminds us of how far we have to go. Never once does he say, "Look over your shoulder and see how far you've come!"

President Thomas S. Monson reminded us that one of God's greatest gifts to us is the joy of trying again. With that gift, we know that no failure ever needs to be final (see *Church News*, July 17, 1999).

No failure ever needs to be final because our loving Father in Heaven has put Jesus Christ in charge. The plan They set forth for us is perfect. And part of that occurs because while we're not yet perfect, we have the potential to become like Him. And His greatest desire is that we gradually grow to become more like Him so that we can eventually return to live with Him (see Boyd K. Packer, "To Young Women and Men," *Ensign*, May 1989, 54).

It's easy to buy into Satan's strategy. He discourages us. He distracts us. This is how he defeats us, for discouragement and distraction rob us of hope—and without hope, "ye must needs be in despair" (Moro. 10:22).

Life has not been easy for me and I suspect it hasn't been easy for you. It wasn't designed that way. Still, it's unfortunate, even tragic, when Latter-day Saints lose hope. I've walked out of church meetings so discouraged that I could not hold my head up. Why? Because I've fallen far short of the standard set forth in the lessons taught. I've berated myself as I've heard sisters tell of their predawn exercise routines, their no-fat, low-carb diets, their faithful husbands and obedient children. Sometimes I've even let the unkind words or harsh judgments of others infect my spirit. I've asked myself, *What is wrong with me?* I've chided myself for failing, when really, I haven't failed at all! The mere fact that I'm at church, trying, means I haven't failed. Do I want to improve? Of course I do. I want to be the best me possible.

A few years ago, after a heartbreaking divorce, I wrote a book entitled *Defined By Christ*. It addresses the fact that Christ alone has the right to define us. His is the defining voice that we should believe and heed. I've never received such heartfelt response for one of my works. It's not because of me; rather, it's because of the message. *Refined by Christ* takes us a step further. It addresses not only who we are in the eyes of God, but also who He sees us becoming. It's a journey of hope and happiness. It's preventive spiritual medicine: It's one thing to know who we are in the eyes of our Savior; it is quite another to do something about it. Something great.

Can't you feel a warmth burning within you, reminding you that you are a child of a God who knows you, loves you, expects wondrous things from you? You were born into this life equipped to succeed. You are a part of God's perfect plan. Yes, you. The plan would not be perfect if you were missing. Think about that. You matter more than you know.

There is a plaque in our home with a quote attributed to President Gordon B. Hinckley: *Try a little harder to be a little better.* There is no aspect of our lives to which that admonishment does not apply. I can pray and read the scriptures *a little better*, I can serve my neighbor *a little better*, I can make a meal *a little better*, I can wash the car *a little better*, I can exercise *a little better*, I can teach a class or engineer a rocket ship *a little better*. Okay, so I can't engineer a rocket ship at all. You get the idea.

The Holy Spirit didn't send me back to embrace that Indian woman so that *she* would be blessed. He sent me back so that we both would be blessed, so that I could do the work I'd come to do *a little better*.

When I was finally obedient, a change happened within me. President Dieter F. Uchtdorf said that something wonderful happens to us as we extend our hands and hearts in Christlike love to others: we ourselves are healed and we become more refined, more peaceful, stronger, happier, and more capable of heeding the whisperings of the Spirit (see "You Are My Hands," *Ensign*, May 2010, 70, 75).

Read that quote again, and pause on the word *refined*. It's a word that appears approximately fifteen times in scripture. It's a word that we must understand if we are to understand ourselves. It's a process we must go through if we are to become spiritually healthy, pure, and powerful.

Not for Amateurs

No, life was not designed to be easy. Just when we overcome one challenge another one is set before us. This experience is not for amateurs. Good thing we are not amateurs. Whether we recognize it or not, we are seasoned spirits. We lived for countless days in the presence of our Creator and our Savior. We learned. We grew. We prepared. In a perfect plan, timing is flawless. We were not sent too early or too late. We did not arrive incomplete. Though it may seem like it at times, we did not come to this earth as novices. We came as children of God cloaked in mortality and ability to succeed.

How important is mortality? Our thoughts and actions here determine where and how we will spend the rest of eternity. Elder Joseph B. Worthlin compared this eternal journey to three laps around a track: "We have completed the first lap successfully and have made wonderful progress. We have started on the second lap" ("The Time to Prepare," *Ensign*, May 1998). He then asks us why we allow ourselves to get distracted instead of completing the third lap around the track.

No one can count the days of our probation. The rich man in the Lord's parable certainly thought he would live long enough to build bigger barns to house his overflowing crops. "But God said unto him, Thou fool, this night thy soul shall be required of thee: then whose shall those things be, which thou hast provided?" (Luke 12:20).

Every day is precious. Every decision matters. Now is the time to determine what kind of lives we want to live—not just now, but forever. I, for one, grew tired of living a life I knew was below my potential. I was weary of feeling depressed and defeated. Yes, I had reasons to feel that way, but I did not have the right. As a child of God I don't need to compare myself to anyone else. God has not asked me to run someone else's race. He's set a personal course for me, wrought with specific challenges. I have limitations that others may not. He takes that into account. I have blessings that others do not. Those are counted in the equation.

My God does not judge me in comparison to someone else, and I shouldn't judge myself that way. Instead, I should simply try to outrun and outdo myself. I should learn from today and make tomorrow better. At our spiritual best we are a brew of splendid flaws and unspeakable potential. It's what makes the human experience one of excitement and expectation. It's what makes us both vulnerable and compassionate. Such a balance comes only through a meticulous process known to separate the bleakest parts of us from our brightest.

Refiner's Fire

A phrase in Malachi 3:2 that refers to the Lord as a refiner has become somewhat of an obsession with me. It has led me to study metallurgy, to understand the process that takes a hunk of ugly ore and transforms it into something pure and precious. Unlike smelting or calcining, which involve a chemical change to the raw material, refining only makes purer what was already there. It's a complicated and exciting process—transformation at its magical best. In my layman's terms, it involves the needed materials, heat, filtration, infinite amounts of patience, caustic acid, more heat, more filtration, more patience, molding, more heat, and a final separation and settling to see what the ore has really become.

Relating the refining process to my own life has changed the way I see myself. It's changed the way I feel about adversity. It's given me a renewal of hope; I know it can do the same for you. We are in the great Refiner's care.

One day my son came home from school with a question: "What does God do for a living?"

"He creates," I said.

My son frowned. "I thought He saves people. That's what the scriptures say His work is."

That's exactly right. To Moses the Lord explained, "this is my work and my glory—to bring to pass the immortality and eternal life of man" (Moses 1:39).

Knowing what He does for a living should set us all at peace. We are in God's hands. We can't come up with a surprise big enough or a sin vile enough to thwart His plan. If we allow Him to refine us, we will inevitably end up free from the impurities that separate us from Him. Once the process is complete we will be not 99 percent pure but 100 percent pure, worthy of the greatest gift even God can give: eternal life.

His Image

But what about *now*—right this minute? I'm a sinner. I'm flawed. I am still that ugly piece of ore that seems valueless. What can I do to join forces with the Great Refiner? How can I present myself to Him to get the refining process started? What happens in the interim? And what can I expect once it is over?

I'm excited to explore the possibilities together. *Together* is another word we have to bank on. Our Father has given us agency.

It is one of His great gifts to us. He will never force us to refine our lives. He will work with us and through us. The choice will always be ours. But the result will be His. We must work together.

A story is told of a woman who came across that same verse in Malachi. Like me, she didn't understand what it meant, so she made an appointment with a silversmith. She mentioned nothing of her biblical question, and the silversmith assumed that she was simply curious to see how ore can be refined into silver.

The refiner held a piece of metal to the flame and allowed it to heat up. He explained that the hottest spot was in the center of the flame and that's where the metal must be held for the impurities to be burned away. The woman thought how God holds us to the hottest part of the flames to burn the impurities out of us. The process began to make spiritual sense to her. She could see why the Lord is referred to as a refiner and purifier.

The process took a long time and seemed tedious. She finally asked, "Is it necessary to sit here the entire time the metal is being refined?"

The man became very serious. "Without a doubt," he said. "I must keep my eye on the heated metal the entire time. You see, if it's left in the refining fire one moment too long, it can become unworkable, even destroyed."

Personal revelation flooded this woman's mind. She thought of a loving Father in Heaven who waits with infinite patience before the flames while our impurities are being refined.

"How do you know when the process is complete and the silver is fully refined?" she asked.

Without taking his eyes away from his work, he smiled. "I know it is ready when I can see my image reflected in it."

Held to the Fire

Latter-day Saint children sing a song that proclaims to the world that we are "trying to be like Jesus." Our anthem is our identity: "I am a child of God." When we aren't singing those truths, are we living like children of God? Are we really trying to be like Jesus?

I want to follow His footsteps, so I say. But I seldom want to do the hard thing. I want to stay clear of the refining flames. Yet I'm learning lessons that take me closer and closer to the heat. One of those lessons took me to the other side of a leper colony. The Refiner is teaching me that to get where He is I must go where He has gone. Christ went all the way to Calvary. Before that He made a stop in a Garden where He atoned for my sins, my slothfulness, my suffering. He paid a price I cannot comprehend.

I don't suppose He felt like bleeding from every pore. He did it anyway. I can't imagine that He enjoyed being spit upon, mocked, having nails driven through His flesh and sinew. I don't suppose He was in the mood to be crucified. Yet, He did the hardest thing of all because He knew it was the right thing to do. His motives were born of pure love and obedience. Nothing less.

Thankfully, if we take full advantage of that Atonement we will never have to kneel in Gethsemane and have a price extracted from our souls, one that we are not worthy to pay. Why? Because Christ prepaid our return ticket to live with Heavenly Father. He has paid the price and paved the way. What does He ask in return? That we follow Him.

Come with me as we map out a way to do just that. Applying the refining process to our lives, let's navigate every step. Let's discover new and thrilling ways to practice what we preach. Let's be encouraged and enlightened, never discouraged and frightened.

Some days we recognize and rejoice that we've made progress. Other days we stagnate, and a few days we actually regress. During those times we recognize that we aren't giving our best effort because we've given our all and it's just not enough. Our loving Refiner understands those days. He is never ever, not ever, no never, going to be the voice that condemns us. His Spirit will convict us to correct us but it will never condemn us. No. The voice of our Refiner is one of awareness, encouragement, and appreciation for our efforts.

Christ, above all, knows just how hard life can be.

Christ, above all, knows just how high we are capable of soaring when the impurities of mortality no longer weigh us down.

Can you feel the heat burning within you? It's the fire that will make us pure and mold us into something useful and valuable. Can you see before you the bar of God's refining process being raised? If that bar wasn't raised, we would never realize our potential.

Your potential is as limitless as eternity. Believe that. That does not mean you have all of eternity to get started. Today is the day. Now is the time. Believe in yourself. Satan will tell you that you are as "good as you're going to get." That's not true. He'll tell you that you can't change. You can.

The heat is on. The bar is lifted. Your true potential is about to shine as brilliantly as polished silver and gold.

CHAPTER TWO

Needful Things

"Organize yourselves; prepare every needful thing."
—D&C 88:119

A WOMAN IN HAITI WHO has a very special Book of Mormon allowed me to hold it. It doesn't look significant. It's one of millions with a tattered blue paper cover. It's translated into French with some notes in the margins scribbled in Haitian Creole. The woman's name is Petal, and she puts her lips to that worn cover and kisses her scriptures.

On January 12, 2010, Petal came home from a long shift in a day care. Her nine-year-old brother, Robert, was spending the night with her. She put a pan of rice over a flame to cook then went to the back room of her humble concrete home to be with Robert.

"A feeling inside of me rose up and told me to go outside," Petal recalls. "I was busy with Robert, my back ached, and I didn't want to go. I knew my husband would be home soon and I needed to be certain he had something to eat."

And so Petal ignored the prompting she felt.

"Then a voice inside of my head told me to go outside."

Again, she brushed aside the urge and went to chop the hot pepper she'd brought home to season the rice. The voice repeated the warning, and Petal still had the knife in her hand when she obeyed and stepped out her front door on the little stone path that led from the street to her front door. She looked around, confused. Everything and everyone seemed perfectly normal. "But it didn't feel normal," she told me. "I called for Robert to come outside and join me.

"He came but didn't understand why, and I had no good explanation. Then I heard that voice again, clear as I'm talking to you now, telling me to run back inside and get my Book of Mormon. I didn't wait. I ran inside, grabbed the book from a small table by my bed, and ran back outside. That's when it happened."

"It" was a 7.0 earthquake that shuddered and shook the very foundation of Haiti. Homes, including the small concrete one in which Petal and her husband lived, moaned and groaned and broke apart. Terrified and horrified voices screamed as shrill as sirens. Thick gray dust choked the afternoon air. Robert clung to one of Petal's hands while she clutched her scriptures with her other hand.

Those thirty to forty seconds stretched time into an eternity.

When it was over, Petal knew that the Lord was mindful of her. With a gigantic smile stretched across her beautiful face, she testified, "He wanted me to be safe and to have my Book of Mormon. After all, it is my most needful thing."

Nearly three hundred thousand Haitians were killed that day. God cared about every single one of those people because they too are His children. Sometimes our mortal minds cannot answer the question: Why is one person spared and another taken?

Ninety percent of the town in which Petal lived was destroyed. Her husband was injured but survived. Her brother Robert is still too afraid to enter a building and prefers to sleep amidst the mosquitoes and the stars. Her testimony still strengthens me: "If God can speak to me and make me move, then I know that He knows me. He cares about me and about my family. He knows what is most needful."

Gather and Organize

Now that we have decided that we really do want to be better than before, what does that mean? How do we enter and survive the refining process? What is "most needful"? Make a list: a refiner, a refinery, ore, acids of all sorts, containers, fire, filters, blowtorch, water, molds, protective gear, and a how-to manual. All of these things and more are "needful" to refine gold from ore. The process is more complex than I indicate, but the idea is that if we are going to change from something that is impure to something that is pure, we are going to require some equipment.

While I was researching this book, a company contacted me and told me that if I sent them six hundred dollars they would send me a little bread-maker-size refinery. It requires no chemicals and allows me to mix metals and karats and guarantees that even a novice will turn out pure gold every time. All I have to do is drop my grandma's gold necklaces and rings into the box and *voilà*!

I know better.

Refining isn't an easy process. It takes master skill and time and the right equipment. It's an investment Christ is clearly willing to make in us, but are we willing to invest in ourselves? If we are, then we need to understand what Jesus taught when He visited the home of two very different sisters.

At the Feet of the Savior

If you knew that Jesus was coming to your house for lunch tomorrow, what would you do? I'm serious. Think about it. What would you need to accommodate Him properly? What changes would you make to your home? What food would you need to buy and to prepare? Where would you serve Him? What would you wear? Would you invite anyone else to join you?

Let's learn from Martha and her sister, Mary. You know the story of what happened when Jesus visited them. I hadn't heard it quite the way I did when I studied the gospel in Bethany, the small community on the southeastern slope of the Mount of Olives, just outside Jerusalem. It's where Jesus taught the two sisters the same lesson He taught me in India, the same lesson He taught Petal in Haiti, the same lesson we all need to learn if we're going to understand the process of refinement.

In Jewish custom and law hospitality was, and for the most part still is, paramount, not just polite. It's a tremendous *mitzvah* whose violations have actually led to war (see Judg. 19:18–21, 20:24–27).

Luke records that it was Martha's house, so she was the one to receive Jesus upon His arrival. I wonder if her sister, Mary, helped her clean and prepare the home. Did she accompany Martha to the market to purchase food and accompany her back home to prepare the meal, to be ready for the arrival of the Messiah? I know that I would have been a little stressed, probably snapping my household into line, worried about every detail. I'd be asking myself if there was time and money to recarpet or should we just take Jesus out to a nice restaurant?

Not Martha. She knew the Master and realized what an honor it was to have Him in her home. Besides, she didn't have the option of "taking Him out to eat," so she prepared the best she could. Tradition would require that it was she who had to go out and meet Jesus as He approached her gate—and she had to do it with a smile on her face. "Greet each person with a cheerful facial expression" (Mishnah Avot 1:15). I doubt that Christ was alone as His disciples were almost always with Him, not to mention masses of the curious and the believers. Martha was not allowed to ask Him about His teachings, His journey, or any news He might know until she had first met His needs as a weary traveler and guest to her home.

Upon entering the house she certainly offered Him a basin of water to wash His feet, and she likely washed them for Him. Then a meal was spread before Him, most likely comprised of several small dishes and new-baked bread. All this was happening while Martha saw to it that Christ's animals were also being tended to. That was part of the deal.

What was Mary doing at this stage? What right do we have to compare the two sisters? Is one more spiritual than the other? I don't think so. Perhaps she'd been helping all along and once the Savior sat down she folded herself at His feet. Or maybe she hadn't been as helpful to her sister as she might have been. We don't know. But we do know that once Jesus was comfortable in her home, "Martha was cumbered about much serving" (Luke 10:40) while the scriptures record that Mary "also sat at Jesus' feet, and heard his word" (Luke 10:39).

Also sat at his feet. What does that imply? To some it says that Martha had also sat before the Lord for a time but then rose to tend to the chores. That's probable, but it also says *others* were gathered at the feet of Jesus. More guests. More work. More responsibilities for the hostess—Martha. And there was Mary right in the middle, her focus on the face of Christ, her ears not hearing Martha clatter but hearing only what the Master was teaching.

Two thousand years later I can almost feel Martha's stress and frustration. It makes perfect sense to me that she would plead, "Lord, dost thou not care that my sister hath left me to serve alone? bid her therefore that she help me" (Luke 10:40).

Alone? She didn't even have servants to help her?

I can also feel the love of the Savior, the Great Refiner, when He turned to a frenzied Martha and said, "Martha, Martha, thou art careful [worried] and troubled about many things: But one thing is needful: and Mary hath chosen that good part, which shall not be taken away from her" (Luke 10:41–42).

Martha was worried about keeping the law of Moses. She realized there was a dire penalty for not keeping the law, and she knew too that so many eyes were watching her, because it wasn't just any ordinary guest in her house: it was the Nazarene carpenter whose reputation was known throughout all of Palestine. To her, it was much, much more than that. Mary, on the other hand, was adhering to a blossoming law, a law brought by the One who had come to fulfill the old and instate the new law. But that time had not quite come, and Martha was worried about keeping the laws she knew and understood. Any woman knows that when there are hungry guests in her home, it's hard to stay out of the kitchen.

Pay close attention to how Jesus treated Martha.

First, Jesus acknowledged how Martha felt. He did not chide her for her feelings. He understood why she was troubled about many things. She had many responsibilities. But Jesus, the Great Refiner, called her to live above the level she'd set for herself, to hurdle the bar that Jewish society had put into place. He called Martha to do what to her seemed absurdly impossible—to have a seat in her own home and listen to the teachings of the Master while the chores went unattended and empty bellies growled.

Elder Dallin H. Oaks "reminds every Martha, male and female, that we should not be so occupied with what is routine and temporal that we fail to cherish the opportunities that are unique and spiritual" ("Spirituality," *Ensign*, Nov. 1985, 61).

The most "needful" thing was to take advantage of having Jesus there, to sit in His presence and feel of His spirit, to be taught truths from the one who can speak only truth, to be blessed and not just to bless. As the scriptures teach, "there is a time . . . for every purpose and for every work" (Eccl. 1:17).

Did you know that the ancient law also required a certain standard from the guest as well as the host? The guest was to avoid causing the host excess work. A guest was to accede to the host's request. A guest should not bring another along unless informing the host beforehand. He should show gratitude for whatever he received, whether it was much or little.

Jesus kept this law of a gracious guest when He acknowledged Martha's feelings and invited her to partake not of cakes and meat, but of bread that would never leave her hungry and water that would quench her thirst forever. In essence, He asked Martha to rest from her labors and feast on His words.

"One thing is needful," He said. That one thing was Him. It is the very thing He offers to all of us. I'm on Team Martha because I feel for her. I'm on Team Mary because I want to be more like her.

I wonder: Did Martha wipe her hands on her apron and join her sister at the feet of the Master, or did she toss her hands in the air and break into tears of frustration, still worried about the chores that were not done? I hope that she opted for the better part, that which should not be "be taken away from her."

In the end, I like to imagine the dishes left unwashed and the floors left unswept while Martha rested her head on Mary's shoulder at Jesus' feet.

The Right Tools

What is more important than our spiritual development? I can't think of anything. The relationship you develop with your God will be the most important relationship you can possibly cultivate. It will lead to a healthy relationship with *you* and to rewarding, lasting relationships with others. It will lead you to focus on your goals, hope in your trials, and ultimate victory in your journey on this earth. This is the very purpose of the refining process: to develop spirituality. Elder M. Russell Ballard taught that the most important part of life is spiritual growth (see "Spiritual Development," *Ensign*, Nov. 1978).

Because God is a god of order—"Mine house is a house of order" (D&C 132:8)—victory in spiritual development requires that we organize ourselves. "Organize yourselves; prepare every needful thing" (D&C 88:119).

A refiner needs special equipment to refine ore into precious metal, and we need special equipment to become spiritually refined. Things like faith, hope, and charity are not things that can be seen and set on a shelf. I asked fifty people the question, What things are needed for spiritual refinement? Most listed nontangible tools like clean thoughts and a pure heart. Your list of "needful" things might be different from mine, but I suspect some items on our lists will overlap. Once you've made your list, organize those items into ideas and those ideas into a plan. It's one thing to know what is needed; it's quite another thing to actually use it.

An Awareness

Are you aware of who you really are in relationship to the very God who created the universe, who scattered the stars and aligned the planets? The fire of refinement can be welcome only to those who remember and realize that they are literally spirit children of a God who knows and loves them. Otherwise, pain and adversity are just that—pain and adversity. Fire doesn't purify; it only burns.

As parents who want our children to develop testimonies, we do exactly what King Benjamin did. We gather them together and instill in them two main things: our love for them and God's love for them. The reason the people loved King Benjamin so much and believed what he testified to them was because they felt his love for them. His concern for their welfare was genuine. He wanted what was best for them.

King Benjamin explained the plan of salvation in a way that made life make sense. His love, faith, and powerful teaching invited the Holy Ghost, which brought the people to a complete awareness of their nothingness and their worthless and fallen state. But they did not stay in that state one second longer than was necessary because King Benjamin focused not on them but on "the goodness of God."

He gave them hope in their spiritual identity, their value in the eyes of a merciful God. In essence, he held a mirror up so they could all see reflected back at them pieces of ore—then he promised them with power from on high that within that ore was gold and that God was willing to refine it, to change them from something worthless to something of great value—

"… the knowledge of the goodness of God at this time has awakened you to a sense of your nothingness, and your worthless and fallen state—if ye have come to a knowledge of the goodness of God, and his matchless power, and his wisdom, and his patience, and his long-suffering towards the children of men; and also, the atonement which has been prepared from the foundation of the world, that thereby salvation might come to him that should put his trust in the Lord, and should be diligent in keeping his commandments, and continue in the faith even unto the end of his life." (Mosiah 4:5–6)

With a single voice the people cried, "O have mercy, and apply the atoning blood of Christ that we may receive forgiveness of our sins" (Mosiah 4:2).

We have to be aware that we are going through a refining process. We have to be aware that our Refiner loves us, is concerned for our welfare, will do anything it takes to purify us and to return us to the presence of our Father in Heaven. If we keep this awareness at the front of our minds and in the core of our hearts, life will make sense, adversity will be understood, and we can cry for help and relief to the One who is in charge.

Available Resources

The greatest gift you have is life itself; second is the agency to choose. Consider this: those gifts would be worthless without the Atonement of Jesus Christ because we're all going to mess up our choices from time to time. That gives us hope that our lives can become eternal and that our sins and sufferings can be made into something useful and clean.

You have fingerprints and toe prints that are uniquely yours. You are a spiritual snowflake. No one is exactly like you. The One who created and assembled you made you absolutely unique. You have been given gifts that are yours alone. Yes, there are millions and millions of people who are musically or artistically gifted, but they are not gifted in the same way you are. There are minds that are apt at math and minds that cannot even get telephone numbers in proper order. The point is, spiritual refinement requires us to recognize and organize our gifts.

When I first started attending church I squirmed in meetings when the teacher asked us to list our talents. I believed I had no talent. I couldn't sing. I couldn't draw. I couldn't dance or play an instrument. I'd been raised an orphan, in and out of foster care, and I lacked lessons in the very basics. I remember girls laughing at me because no one had ever taught me how to curl my hair or apply makeup. I felt humiliated and worthless.

In time I figured out how to roll my hair in curlers and how to wave a wand of mascara. More importantly, I learned that God didn't send a single soul into this world without a myriad of gifts. Think about your physical body. It was designed by a loving Creator who knew precisely what it needed to function. Ten toes are just the right number of toes to balance us. Two thumbs come in pretty handy—not three or four, but two. Five senses cover everything we need—nothing more, nothing less.

Your physical body is a tremendous gift from a loving Creator. Recognizing it as a gift, learning to care for it in every way, developing it as you develop the spirit it encases, is very much a part of the refining process.

My friend Ammon was born with a body that does not work like mine. His mind is also different. Ammon was born unable to move his arms or legs. His brain did not develop the same way mine did. Ammon cannot form words, but he has learned to communicate with smiles and frowns. His spirit speaks in a way that I cannot explain, but I feel better when I am in Ammon's presence. He is a unique and gifted individual who teaches and inspires simply by existing.

If your body was created with such perfect precision, why wouldn't your spirit be endowed with all that it needs too? It is. The first gift you can count is the Spirit of the Holy Ghost to guide, protect, and comfort you, to remind you who you truly are.

You have a personality that is not a carbon copy of your mother's or your father's personality. You might have shared traits, but not exact traits. Your desires are different, too. So are your ambitions and abilities.

Make a list of the gifts you believe God has given you. Remember, you are never going to be judged or held accountable for someone else's gift, only for the development and use of your own. If you struggle, ask someone who loves you what he or she thinks your gifts are and start there. Better yet, ask the Holy Ghost to enlighten you. Then organize your gifts. Some will be more obvious—"To some is given one, and to some is given another, that all may be profited thereby" (D&C 46:12).

That's the kicker—*that all may be profited thereby.*

How can you use the gifts you've been given to profit others? If you have the gift of faith, your testimony can help others who struggle to believe. "To some it is given by the Holy Ghost to know that Jesus Christ is the Son of God, and that he was crucified for the sins of the world. To others it is given to believe on their words, that they also might have eternal life if they continue faithful" (D&C 46:13–14).

The task is to recognize your gifts and put them in order, to refine them so they can profit both you and others.

A Grateful Heart

Refinement doesn't work if we are not grateful for our Refiner and His work. His work is perfecting and saving us, and unless we are grateful for what He does on our behalf, impurities will never leave us. "Thou shalt thank the Lord thy God in all things. . . . And in nothing doth man offend God, or against none is his wrath kindled, save those who confess not his hand in all things" (D&C 59:7, 21).

A grateful heart is a gift we can pray for if we don't have one. It's something we can cultivate by receiving and acknowledging the source of our blessings. It's more than a thank-you; it's a profound feeling. It's part of faith, believing that God is good, generous, and wants to help. Martha gets a bad rap in the telling of her story. It seems she is not as spiritual as her sister, but it was Martha who ran to meet Jesus "as soon as she heard" He was coming. Her brother, Lazarus, had died days before, and she took her broken, grateful heart to meet the Savior. You might think this part is all about asking, and she does that, but it is one of the most powerful lessons we can learn about gratitude. As Martha meets Jesus she tells Him, "Lord, if thou hadst been here, my brother had not died. But I know, that even now, whatsoever thou wilt ask of God, God will give it thee" (John 11:21–22).

This is her testimony, a powerful expression of gratitude because it's an acknowledgement of who Christ is and how much God loves Him.

Jesus is our Mediator for the Father. He is our Advocate. Until we realize this we cannot begin to understand the love that accompanies the refining process. Until then, all we feel is suffering, and who wants to be grateful for pain?

Because God's ways are not man's ways, one way we can express gratitude is to acknowledge and appreciate what we've already been given. But another way, often overlooked, is to do exactly what Martha did—to ask in faith for what we want and what we need. I'm not talking about a "gimme" attitude; I'm talking about Martha's attitude. She ran to Him in need. She acknowledged His power and goodness.

In return, Jesus taught Martha, "I am the resurrection, and the life: he that believeth in me, though he were dead, yet shall he live: And whosoever liveth and believeth in me shall never die. Believest thou this?" (John 11:25–26).

She responded with her testimony: "Yea, Lord: I believe that thou art the Christ, the Son of God, which should come into the world" (John 11:27).

When is the last time you bore your testimony to the Savior about the Savior?

Pay close attention to what Christ does next, because it teaches us another new lesson about gratitude: "Then they took away the stone from the place where the dead was laid. And Jesus lifted up his eyes, and said, Father, I thank thee that thou hast heard me" (John 11:41).

Jesus thanked his Father while Lazarus was still dead. In other words, He thanked Him first, before the miracle. This was what Martha was doing—acknowledging the power and goodness of God. It's what we all should do.

Time

Stop being the Chief Everything Officer—don't say yes by default. It's a hard lesson to learn but in order to be wickedly successful, you have to understand that by saying no to some things you will have the time and energy to say yes to the right things. If you're feeling overwhelmed and pulled in every direction, you won't be able to lead yourself, much less anyone else.

We are under covenant to be a service-oriented people. That does not mean we are obligated to give our energy to every person or situation that demands it. Keep the end goal in mind. Don't ever leave yourself off the list of your own priorities.

A Purpose, a Cause, a Passion

Once we are aware of who we are in the eyes of God, our worth in His heart, then what? Once we become aware of how gifted we are, the potential that lies within us, then what? We'd better figure out what to do with those gems.

What's your purpose on earth? I can tell you it is to fulfill your second-estate duties—to obtain a body, to be tried and tested, to pass the obedience challenges, to take full advantage of the Atonement—but that's not my place. It's your place. Figure out your purpose like you figured out your gifts—with the help of the Holy Ghost. Talk it over with the Lord. Edit as directed.

Now figure out your cause. It's different than your purpose. Your purpose is the reason you're here. Your cause is what you're going to do about it. My cause is to testify of God the Father. Period. How I do it varies as the Lord refines me and streamlines my life. I am in a continuous process of refinement. That doesn't matter. My cause stays the same.

Finally, figure out your passion. What floats your boat, rings your bell, lights your tree? A life without passion is possible but not desirable. Have you really lived at all if you have not lived with passion? Without it would a masterpiece be possible? I don't think so. With purpose, cause, and passion, the end you envision will absolutely become the reality you live.

If you have a painting in you, paint. If you have a song to sing, sing. Don't judge your creation. Just create it. Banish doubt and fear and step out of your own way if you have to. Write if you're a writer and invent if you're an inventor. Do what you were born to do. Only then will you know a remarkable life.

Ears to Hear

One night during family prayer my young son petitioned the Lord for a new pair of ears.

"What's wrong with the ones you have?" I asked him.

"They can't always hear the Holy Ghost."

The Lord is speaking to us. He's doing it through scriptures, prophets, leaders, and teachers. He is doing it through whisperings of His Holy Spirit. What does the voice of the Lord sound like? Sometimes it is nothing more than a good feeling, a prompting to do the right thing. Other times it sounds just like the familiar voice of a loving parent or dedicated teacher.

When is the last time we prayed for a new pair of ears—ones attuned to hear the Holy Ghost?

Fast Feet

In the seventeenth chapter of the book of Samuel is the story of a young shepherd boy who gets caught in the middle of a great battle. The people of Saul, king of Israel, stand on one side of the mountain. The Philistines stand on the other. There's a valley between them. All are camped, uncertain of their future.

Saul seems to have forgotten that God is on the side of Israel because he has seen with his own eyes that Goliath is on the side of the Philistines. Goliath, the giant, must have been terrifying; his armor alone is estimated to have weighed more than three hundred pounds. His height was six cubits and a span. (A cubit is the length of a person's forearm from the elbow to the tip of the middle finger—about eighteen inches—and a span is the length between the tip of the thumb and the tip of the little finger when the hand is fully extended, or nine inches. That would have made Goliath nine feet nine inches tall. Archeologists estimate the average height of a man back then would level off around five feet zero inches.)

The challenge is made: If the Israelites can send forth a man capable of killing Goliath, the Philistines will become slaves to them. If Goliath prevails, then Israel will be enslaved to the Philistines. The picture is clear. The army of Israel is in grave trouble. Saul can see no one capable of defeating Goliath, because Saul can't see what God can see. Somewhere in the rocky hills around Bethlehem, God sees a young boy tending to his father's sheep.

For forty days and forty nights the Philistines taunt the Israelites. The two armies are about to go head-to-head when a young boy shows up with some bread and cheese for the hungry captains. He is on his father's errand when he is called to tend to another Father's errand. David leaves his carriage and runs to the army of Israel to three of his own brothers, who are terrified of the oversized Philistine.

David asks, "Who is this uncircumcised Philistine, that he should defy the armies of the living God?" (1 Sam. 17:26).

Then David, called before the king, declares, "Let no man's heart fail because of him; thy servant will go and fight with this Philistine" (1 Sam. 17:32).

David's brothers have already belittled him, and now the king tells David that he is just a young boy who cannot hope to battle Goliath. But David does what we all should do when faced with a refining challenge: He rehearses all the good things the Lord has already done for him. He's already helped David kill a lion and a bear. Of course He'll help him kill an arrogant giant. So Saul agrees and then says in essence, "I'm going to allow you go to because, well, I don't have a lot of other volunteers—but if you're going out there to fight, at least wear my armor."

What Saul is really telling David is, "Do it my way."

David tries to honor his king, but the armor does not fit and will not protect him like the armor of faith. So David does what works for him. He takes off Saul's armor; grabs his staff, his sling, and five smooth stones; and he runs out to fight Goliath.

When the giant sees a fair-faced young boy he is outraged. He mocks David, but David does not lose faith in himself or in His God. He shouts up at Goliath's face, "Thou comest to me with a sword, and with a spear, and with a shield: but I come to thee in the name of the Lord of hosts, the God of the armies of Israel, whom thou hast defied" (1 Sam. 17:45).

Then David does what he ran forth to do. He defends his God by slaying the giant.

Three important things David did are often overlooked: He "got up early" to honor his earthly father's wish to deliver food to the army. When David arrived at the camp, he "ran" to greet his brothers. And when the battle cry sounded, he "ran" toward Goliath.

When the Lord calls us to battle, our feet should be ready to run.

A Destination

It's not enough to be willing to run. We have to have a destination.

In the refining process, ore is destined to become pure gold. In the refining process, frail humans are destined to become pure gods.

You can always edit your list of resources to help you become spiritually refined. I can't tell you what your most "needful" things are. Only you can do that. But I can urge you to get started and to not lose sight of all that you've been given to help you achieve the greatest of all goals—to become pure and able to progress without ceasing.

CHAPTER THREE

Turn Up the Heat

"The glory of this latter house shall be greater
than the former, saith the Lord of hosts."
—Hag. 2:9

WHEN I WAS ABOUT EIGHT years old my grandmother visited from out of town. She helped clean the house, and when she was done she put the mop and broom in a little closet that contained both the hot water heater and the furnace.

Sometime during the night my mother shook me awake and screamed at me to run from the house: The mop and broom had caught fire, and our entire kitchen, dining room, laundry room, and front room were engulfed in flames. Mom wrapped wet towels around me and rushed me down a smoky hallway and into the fresh black air of night. My older brother was already outside with some of our neighbors. Mom went back in to rescue our little dog. I tried to run in after her because I'd left my doll, Betsy, beneath the covers where I'd been sleeping.

I remember standing there in the street looking at the faces of neighbors and strangers as they watched our home burn. I will never forget the terror I felt, worrying that Mom would not emerge safely. She finally did, and in her arms was our trembling little dog that had been hiding underneath one of the beds.

"Where's Betsy?" I sobbed.

"Oh, Toni."

I was too young to realize the destruction and danger of such a fire. It all seemed so spectacular and dramatic. A kind neighbor took me to her home where I slept fitfully, without my beloved doll, until the next morning. In the light of day nothing seemed spectacular or dramatic. It was nothing more than an ashy, still-smoldering graveyard. It was so foreign to me that the firemen in yellow suits and big black helmets reminded me of spacemen on the moon.

Mother seemed relieved and worried at the same time. She kept hugging me and weeping. I was glad my family was okay—even my big brother, who seemed as fine as ever. But what about Betsy? The firemen said I would have to wait to look for her.

Part of our home was still standing, but part was burned to the ground. The fish tank in the living room was intact, and the piranhas that Mother kept appeared undisturbed, though I'm sure the temperature in their tank rose in all the heat. (Yes, that's right—piranhas—prehistoric man-eating fish. But that's a different story for a different time.)

I was not permitted to sift through the ruins until later that afternoon. My ceiling was now a cloudy gray sky; the floor of ashes and soot was warm to the soles of my borrowed shoes, for I wore things that came from the kindness of strangers. It was difficult to even tell where my room had been. My bed was just a still-warm metal frame, the mattress a square of ugly black puff. A charred metal pole let me know where my closet had been, but almost all of my clothes were burned to ashes. What the flames didn't consume the fire-hose water ruined.

The thing I looked for first and most desperately was my doll, Betsy, who'd been purchased at ZCMI for twenty whole dollars—an absurd sum of money back then. She had thick black eyelashes, chopped in an even row. Her eyes were blue marbles that moved when she was tilted so that it seemed she was looking around. That seems kind of creepy now, but back then it made Betsy seem real—

that, along with the fact that she cried when I cradled her, and water ran right through her when I gave her a bottle. I don't know how many times I changed that damp little pink ruffled diaper of hers.

Something hard pressed beneath my foot. A mass of rocklike plastic.

"Oh no!" my mother said, leaning to pick it up.

That's when I saw a single blue marble that had been one of Betsy's eyes.

I must have cried for weeks. My Betsy Wetsy doll, once so perfect and precious, was now a charred lump of melted plastic.

Many years later I found myself the single mother of a houseful of children. It now fell solely to me to support them in every single way, including financially. I wasn't doing such a terrific job. As we approached the Thanksgiving holiday season there was more month than money, and the power company threatened to turn off our heat. I called and told them that I would have a paycheck in a few days. I asked them to trust me and promised to get them the funds right after Thanksgiving.

To be honest, I was distraught and distracted and didn't think they'd really turn off our heat over the holidays. Turns out whoever was in charge of that power switch had a Grinch of a heart because our power went out and with it our heat.

It wasn't the end of the world. A friend supplied us with wood, and the kids made a fire in the fireplace. We gathered our blankets and bundled together around the flames. That experience made for one of the most memorable holidays ever. We still talk about it, and I will never forget how grateful I was for the warmth and light of fire.

How can fire be both productive and destructive? You know the answer. Fire, like anything with such power, has to be contained and controlled.

Why So Hot?

Consider Nephi in the wilderness. He was given the task of constructing a ship to cross the great ocean to the promised land. I suppose he already knew something of metallurgy or perhaps the Lord gave him a crash course. Either way, he records:

> The voice of the Lord came unto me, saying: Arise, and get thee into the mountain. And it came to pass that I arose and went up into the mountain, and cried unto the Lord.
>
> And it came to pass that the Lord spake unto me, saying: Thou shalt construct a ship, after the manner which I shall show thee, that I may carry thy people across these waters.
>
> And I said: Lord, whither shall I go that I may find ore to molten, that I may make tools to construct the ship after the manner which thou hast shown unto me?
>
> And it came to pass that the Lord told me whither I should go to find ore, that I might make tools.
>
> And it came to pass that I, Nephi, did make a bellows wherewith to blow the fire, of the skins of beasts; and after I had made a bellows, that I might have wherewith to blow the fire, I did smite two stones together that I might make fire. (1 Ne. 17:7–11)

Two stones to make fire. A bellows to blow air to make the fire hot enough to melt ore. I was a Cub Scout leader; I knew how to make a fire by hitting two stones together (not that I ever have). Making a bellows? Not a clue. So I researched and discovered that Nephi had to have appropriate animal skins, large enough to make a bellows. That meant he had to hunt, kill, skin the beast(s), and cure and dry that skin. Hard, flat sides had to be made, probably out of wood. Handles had to be designed and constructed as well as a nozzle through which the air could pass. Archeological evidence suggests that blacksmiths in the Middle East were smelting iron as early Lehi's expedition, but even if Nephi knew something of metallurgy and refining, it didn't make his task easy. It was difficult and complicated, and it would not be included in the Book of Mormon if it wasn't relevant to us today. We needed to know not just the fact that he was willing to do what the Lord required, but also how it was accomplished and why it was necessary to do it at all.

First, the Lord called Nephi to go to the mountain. He went without question. There Nephi cried unto the Lord, and the Lord gave him the news about their needing a ship to cross the ocean. Nephi didn't panic. He asked the Lord where to go to find ore to molten to make the tools to make the ship. The Lord showed Nephi where to find the needed ore. This is a big deal because we have to know that the Lord knows where the gold is, especially the gold deep within us.

Then Nephi made a bellows, and he made fire. An open fire does not burn hot enough to melt ore, so Nephi had to construct some type of burning chamber or furnace—a kiln, if you will. Primitively, blacksmiths burned charcoal with iron ore and a good supply of oxygen (provided by the bellows). Charcoal, essentially pure carbon, combines with oxygen to create carbon dioxide and carbon monoxide, releasing impressive amounts of heat. To obtain the iron in the ore, it has to be heated until the metal becomes spongy and the chemical compounds in the ore begin to break down.

It's very difficult to get the fire hot enough to completely melt the iron. The mass is heated and hammered, forcing the impurities out and mixing the glassy silicates into the iron metal to create what we call wrought iron—perfect for making the kind of tools Nephi would have required. Wrought iron for crude tool-making requires the iron be heated hot enough to make it spongy and to soften it—not to melt it completely. It's useful and relatively valuable, but it certainly isn't pure. So the hotter the heat, the purer the metal—but even that must be controlled, because metal heated too hot or left too long in the heat can be destroyed.

When the Heat Is On

Think of you and of me as clumps of ore. Inside us are veins of pure gold, a little silver, some copper, and some other less-precious metals. In order to get out what's valuable deep within us, we have to go through a refiner's fire. The good, the bad, and the ugly are melted together. At first it's horrific. Then the heat grows hotter, and we turn soft and sort of spongy, pliable, and workable. We're still not pure—not by a long shot. We're still speckled with imperfections and impurities, prone to attract bits and pieces of rock and metal that take us back a step or two. But if we let the Refiner turn up the heat, trusting that He will be there to watch us with love and care, we can and will become pure and valuable beyond measure.

That all sounds good, but what's the heating process really like? Are you familiar with a promise that God will never allow your burden to be heavier than you can bear? I've heard that taught a dozen different ways. But is it true? To get this, most Christians refer to 1 Corinthians 10:13: "There hath no temptation taken you but such as is common to man: but God is faithful, who will not suffer you to be tempted above that ye are able; but will with the temptation also make a way to escape, that ye may be able to bear it."

People have told me this when I have been in agony. I've told people the same thing but now I understand the concept so differently because I understand how the Lord works in His role as refiner and purifier.

Temptation is a test of someone's ability to choose good over evil. Temptation is a part of the perfect plan. What's the difference between a temptation and a trial? A trial might be a disappointment, heartbreak, illness, sadness, loss, or adversity of any kind. With the help of the Lord, trials can lead to spiritual growth, refinement, and progress. Trials are also part of a perfect plan but they are not the same as temptations, so the scripture isn't promising that we won't be given more trials than we can bear. It simply isn't.

From the apostle's own words to his brothers in Corinth, "For we would not, brethren, have you ignorant of our trouble which came to us in Asia, that we were pressed out of measure, above strength, insomuch that we despaired even of life" (2 Cor. 1:8).

We worship Jesus Christ—our Savior, our Advocate, the Refiner of our lives—because He truly can empathize with both the temptations we face and the trials that weigh us down. It is He who has made one promise clarion: "Come unto me, all ye that labour and are heavy laden, and I will give you rest. Take my yoke upon you, and learn of me; for I am meek and lowly in heart: and ye shall find rest unto your souls. For my yoke is easy, and my burden is light" (Matt. 11:28–30).

How can His burden be light and His yoke easy when our trials are so heavy and hard? There is no burden heavier than the burden of sin. Its weight has worn me down and worn me out. Only when I turn it over to the One who has already borne it for me do I feel free.

As for the weight of our trials, Christ has "borne our griefs, and carried our sorrows," Isaiah declared, "and with his stripes we are healed"—if we want to be and if we are willing to do what He asks of us (Isa. 53:4–5; see also Mosiah 14:4–5).

How does this bearing our griefs, lifting our sorrows, and healing us happen? I lived as a member of the Church for decades before I recognized this power in my life. I was driving along a busy road one day when I received a cell phone call telling me some heartbreaking news. I pulled the car off to the side of the road and felt as though the weight of the entire car was on my chest. I bowed my head and prayed, "Father, I come to Thee because I can't do this. I'm already carrying more than I can bear. I cannot carry the weight of this new burden. Please, I beg, take it from me."

I testify to you that in the exact moment of "Amen," I felt an actual weight lifted. I could breathe. I could smile. I could pull the car back into the flow of traffic. That burden did not go away, but the weight of it was lifted from me. Never once has it returned.

My experience is more beautifully taught in the Book of Mormon when the wicked priest Amulon began to persecute the people of Alma, exercising authority over them and putting tasks upon them that brought great afflictions. They prayed mightily to God, even when they could only do it through "the thoughts of their hearts."

"And it came to pass that the voice of the Lord came to them in their afflictions, saying: Lift up your heads and be of good comfort. . . . I will also ease the burdens which are put upon your shoulders, that even you cannot feel them upon your backs, even while you are in bondage; and this will I do that ye may stand as witnesses for me hereafter, and that ye may know of a surety that I, the Lord God, do visit my people in their afflictions" (Mosiah 24:13–14).

If we want our burdens to refine us and not destroy us, we must cry out to God and do it mightily. It works. I promise it works.

Knowing the Refiner

The key to enduring the heat is to know the nature of the Refiner. The Prophet Joseph Smith taught in *Lectures on Faith* that it is necessary to have "an acquaintance" with the divine attributes of the Father and the Son so that we can have faith in Them. If we do not believe that our Refiner is refining us out of love and a longing for us to return to live with Heavenly Father, then the heat only blisters and burns; it does not refine.

We must believe that the Lord is "merciful and gracious, slow to anger, long-suffering and full of goodness," unless we can rely on "the excellency" of the Savior's character, unless we do not doubt that He can and will "forgive iniquity, transgression, and sin," Joseph taught that we will remain "in constant doubt of salvation" (*Lectures on Faith* [1985], 41–42).

When the fire gets too hot and threatens to destroy us, Jesus Christ is the one who can rescue us. He can turn down the temperature, or take us all the way out of the furnace—or he can leave us in the flames but stay beside us.

Think of Nebuchadnezzar, great king of Babylon, who got wind of three Jews who refused to fall down and worship the golden image commissioned by the king. It was no little calf, but a hand-crafted idol ninety feet high and nine feet wide. Upon the sound of a specific blend of musical instruments, the subjects of the land were ordered to bow down and worship the idol. But Shadrach, Meshach, and Abed-nego wouldn't bow down.

They were brought before an incensed king. He asked, in other words, "Is it true, Shadrach, Meshach, and Abed-nego, that you don't serve my gods or worship the golden image I have set up?"

Nope. No way. They were not about to bow before an idol. They worshipped and served the God of Israel.

What happened to these good young men when they stood up for truth and testimony? The mean old king put them into a furnace and turned the heat up seven notches. Seven times hotter for doing what was right. Tell me how that is fair.

But when the king peered into the furnace, what did he see? A fourth person in the furnace with them—right in the flames *with* them. He told those assembled, "Lo, I see four men loose, walking in the midst of the fire, and they have no hurt; and the form of the fourth is like the Son of God" (Dan. 3:25).

Jesus Christ is our Refiner. He knows the heat of the furnace because He has been in the furnace, and He knows how to refine us through it.

What about the prophet Abinadi? He was tortured to death with fire (see Mosiah 17:20). Why was he allowed to die when the three young Israelites were spared even a singe or the smell of smoke? I don't think *why* should occupy our minds—instead, we need to think about *who*. *Who* was Abinadi testifying of? *Who* did he believe in? *Who* granted agency—not only to the righteous, like Abinadi, but also to the murderous priests? *Who*, less than two hundred years later, would do the same for Abinadi—not by fire, but by crucifixion?

Others were martyred by fire in the scriptures, and though we have no written record of Christ being with them as He was with those in Nebuchadnezzar's furnace, we have to believe Jesus when He vows, "Lo, I am with you alway, even unto the end of the world" (Matt. 28:20).

Paul's Perspective

Go back to Paul's letter to his brothers in Corinth. Keep in mind he is a man of astounding faith and fortitude. He's already been refined from an unbelieving Saul to an unwavering Paul. Before he addressed the trouble that made him despair, he wrote, "Blessed be God, even the Father of our Lord Jesus Christ, the Father of mercies, and the God of all comfort" (2 Cor. 1:3).

Paul knew what we know: that God comforts us when we seek Him in our trials. He lifts our burdens and eases our pain.

"Who comforteth us in all our tribulation" (2 Cor. 1:4)? The word *all* strikes me because sometimes I'm in pain as the result of making a stupid decision or tampering with a commandment. It's easy for me to pray for comfort when someone else has hurt me, but when I've brought the pain on by my own actions or decisions, I don't feel so worthy of comfort. Yet God comforteth us in *all* our tribulation, "that we may be able to comfort them which are in any trouble, by the comfort wherewith we ourselves are comforted of God" (2 Cor. 1:4).

Finally, parts of my life began to make sense. The Lord had comforted me through some pretty horrible times, and now He expected me to comfort others. I found I could listen to an abused child and feel his pain because I had once been that child. I could hold a woman who had lost a child because I had lost a child. I could encourage a woman in the midst of divorce because I had made it to the other side. Unless you've experienced the word *cancer*, you cannot truly understand the fear it wields. If you've never worked outside the home, the pain and guilt of leaving your family isn't real. It's not that others cannot feel sympathy, but they cannot know empathy. Never forget that Jesus Christ could have received an understanding of human suffering through revelation; instead, He chose to receive it through life and suffering and sorrow so that He would know how to succor us. That's how much He loves us.

"Our hope of you is stedfast, knowing, that as ye are partakers of the sufferings, so shall ye be also of the consolation" (2 Cor. 1:7). We can all take hope when the heat intensifies. Yes, we will suffer, but there is comfort and consolation from the Refiner Himself.

"For we would not, brethren, have you ignorant of our trouble which came to us in Asia, that we were pressed out of measure, above strength, insomuch that we despaired even of life" (2 Cor. 1:8). Trials were so great that Paul wasn't sure he could live through them. His hardships were more than he could humanly handle. Most of us can relate to this kind of despair. Other translations of the Bible read: "utterly burdened beyond our strength" (ESV) and "crushed and completely" (NLT).

"But we had the sentence of death in ourselves, that we should not trust in ourselves, but in God which raiseth the dead" (2 Cor. 1:9). Paul and his companions learned that none of us can survive when we are spiritually self-sufficient, because there is no such thing. Our trials force us to rely on God. Paul's despair might have brought him to death's door, but he knew that even in death there was One who could break that door down and raise him again.

Melting Pot

As we begin the refining process we are very much like Paul. We have strength yet we have weakness. We have faith yet we experience doubt. We are part saint and part sinner. Everything we are, everything we are not, all goes into the crucible to be melted together. The gold in us can only be separated through refinement. Refinement means fire.

I think of my Betsy doll. Fire destroyed her. No matter how I wailed, the firemen could not fix her. My mother could not fix her. My brother didn't want to. I couldn't. I sometimes think of myself as Betsy—a big, unidentifiable mess, beyond repair or restoration. Yet God can see in me what others cannot. He knows I have worth. He knows I have potential. And He knows that without Him I will remain that hopeless mess. But with His grace and mercy, with His refining Atonement burning brightly, fire will not destroy me but will purify and make possible what seemed so impossible.

CHAPTER FOUR

*"No experience in life is ever wasted—no matter the outcome,
good or bad—if you learn from it in the end."*
—Unknown

IT'S A REWARDING BLESSING TO be able to volunteer at the Missionary
Training Center (MTC), where I get to role play in different foreign
languages. Sometimes I own a *mercado* and get to sell *plátanos* to the
elders. Or I might be the proprietor of a French bakery that feeds
hungry missionaries a *pâtisserie* or *deux*. Other times they pretend to
meet me at a park, on a bus, or at the front door of my own apartment.
One day I was told to simply be myself and to answer the questions
honestly and respond from the circumstances of my own life.

"Tell us about yourself," two elders, one from Alabama and one
from Idaho, asked.

"I'm a mom and a writer," I said.

"What about your husband? What does he do for a living?"

"I'm divorced."

The smiles fell from their faces.

"How long were you married before your divorce?" the sweet
elder from Alabama ventured to ask.

"Twenty-four years."

He groaned and leaned back in his chair. His hand slapped his
forehead. "I'm so sorry for you. Think of all those wasted years."

To Waste or Not to Waste

That elder spoke aloud a thought that had plagued me for a long time. Had I wasted much of my life giving everything to a marriage that failed?

I don't think so, and the reason I don't think so can be summed up in one word familiar to every refiner: *slag.*

This is the part of the process when we begin to see and feel a true separation between the result and the rest. Slag is a vitreous (glassy) byproduct left as a residue when refining metallic ore—a separation occurs, and the undesired impurities rise to the top.

Think of it as the opposite of separating milk from cream. In that process, cream—the richest part of the product—rises to the top while the rest stays below. In the refinery process, gold—the richest part of the product—is nineteen times heavier than water, so it sinks to the bottom while the slag rises to the top.

But don't assume that because slag is something less than gold, it has no purpose and is worthless. No. No. No. Any oxygen that gets through causes metals to oxidize; slag serves as a protective crust of oxides, providing a protective "lid" for the liquid metal beneath. It serves in this capacity and so much more.

Every year hundreds of tons of slag are produced in refineries. After it is skimmed from the top of the melted liquid, the slag is put into a heap, where it ages. It is important to allow it to cool properly and to expose the slag to weather so it will be broken down a bit to be most workable.

At this stage the slag is often dark and crumbly and looks like a loose collection of lumpy aggregate. Wise refiners have found many uses for slag: among other things, it's an ingredient in concrete and aggregate road materials; it is used as ballast; and it is sometimes used as a component of phosphate fertilizer.

Gather the Fragments

What about the slag in my life? I picture my heap to be pretty ugly and pretty large. Fortunately, Jesus covered this concern beautifully and thrillingly in an example from His own life.

His popularity grew great when word of the miracles He performed became known. People came as spectators. They carried their sick and diseased loved ones. They came with sorrows and secrets known only in their hearts. Christ, a god of perfect compassion, could not turn them away.

There is a hill just up from the Sea of Galilee, where Jesus once walked on water. A hot sun reflects off the sparkling water while patches of purple, pink, blue, and yellow wildflowers dot the speckled green hill. On this crest is where I picture Jesus as He looks and sees five thousand men trudging toward Him during Passover—a holy day to feast and to commemorate the Lord's mercy to those children who were "passed over" and to those Israelites who were rescued from slavery.

Christ turns to Phillip and asks, "Whence shall we buy bread, that these may eat?" (John 6:5).

Jesus didn't pose the question because He was worried about bread or lack of bread. The scriptures tell us that He already knew where the bread was going to come from, but He posed the question anyway, to "prove" His disciples. They'd witnessed their Master perform mighty miracles. They knew His divine identity. Still, they were practical people, and if Jesus wanted to observe the Passover feast with such a large crowd, they were going to need more than a few loaves of bread.

"Philip answered him, Two hundred pennyworth of bread [estimated to be eight month's wages] is not sufficient for them, that every one of them may take a little" (John 6:7).

Andrew, Simon Peter's brother, did a frantic search and reported, "There is a lad here, which hath five barley loaves, and two small fishes: but what are they among so many?" (John 6:9).

Jesus must have smiled as He instructed His disciples to have His company take a seat on the grassy hill. Then "Jesus took the loaves; and when he had given thanks, he distributed to the disciples, and the disciples to them that were set down; and likewise of the fishes as much as they would" (John 6:11).

With Jesus as the host the multitude ate first and ate until they were full. "When they were filled, he said unto his disciples, Gather up the fragments that remain, that nothing be lost" (John 6:12).

In so many words, He told them to skim the slag and put the leftovers in Tupperware. And when "they gathered them together [they] filled twelve baskets with the fragments of the five barley loaves, which remained over and above unto them that had eaten" (John 6:13).

I love this story, because it demonstrates powerfully that Jesus is a fabulous host and a mighty miracle worker—and don't overlook the fact that He is no waster. In His own life, every decision mattered, every day counted. Everything Jesus said or did—all of His learning, experience, parables, and sermons—pointed to His divine identity and His saving purpose.

What about the bad days when people mocked Him or turned away? What of the day when He had to actually flee His own home town? Weren't those times for nothing? Not at all. Christ made everything count, including the behavior of others who set out to harm Him or trip Him up. Those things backfired and only served to testify who Jesus, stepson of a carpenter, Son of the Living God, was and is.

That well-meaning missionary at the MTC was wrong. The years I put into a marriage that ended in divorce were not wasted. I have children that I love, children who give my life purpose and passion. I have lessons learned. I have experiences that made me grow and change. I don't have to feel horrible that I failed, because I didn't fail at all. The slag from my mistakes, when in the Refiner's care, can be used to build new roads to a better, brighter future.

Utah's Gold Rush

In 1847 when the Mormon pioneers first entered Utah Territory, they broke the trail for a massive wave of migration to the region and beyond. The man who led this brave brigade west denounced mining and prospecting for precious metals. Brigham Young instead urged his followers to engage in more "productive" pursuits that would build the kingdom of God. He encouraged the Saints to settle their communities and to build homes, churches, temples. Agriculture was high on President Young's list of priorities; so was the establishment of schools and businesses. The kind of mining he approved of involved minerals required for industry—minerals like coal, iron, lead, sulfur, and salt.

Three years later, a group traveling to California discovered gold in southwestern Utah. Indians had to fight off the mining prospectors. The allure proved worth the danger, and the miners were dogged in their lust for gold. One particular town was built around the gold and silver mines that were established in the area. Men made and lost great fortunes, and the town seemed to blossom overnight with hotels and boarding houses, financial institutions, churches and meeting places, restaurants, and a dry-goods store called The Golden Rules Store—a store that later became JC Penney.

That town and areas all around it yielded rich deposits of silver ore and some gold, though the gold at that time was almost impossible to separate from the rock. Then in 1890 a cyanide leaching process was discovered that allowed extraction of the previously abandoned deposits. Over the next decade, that town and its surrounding areas yielded millions of tons of gold ore. A day's horse-and-buggy ride away in the Oquirrh Mountains, eight million dollars worth of gold was produced.

One of the miners who made a fortune from Utah gold once said, "The earth is the Lord's bank, and no man has a right to take money out of that bank and use it extravagantly upon himself." That man—Jesse Knight, who had crossed the plains—went on to become the patron saint of BYU and one of the most generous donors in the history of the Church (see *Utah's Mining History* [U. S. Press, 1929], 477).

In that small mining town, which was the hub of Jesse Knight's mining empire, a mountain of slag was cast aside, becoming nothing more than a reminder of the Gold Rush days and a repulsive eyesore.

Gold production wound down during World War I. Men were called away, and women worked farms and factories. During the trials of the Great Depression men again searched Utah's hills and mountains for gold. Most had little or no respect for the land and caused significant environmental damage. Then came another World War, and gold mining was declared off-limits by the War Production Board until the war's end.

After that, most of the small mines were abandoned. Today the industry belongs to big business—but for seven decades that mountainous pile of slag in one little town stood as a reminder of the days of pack mules and gold nuggets.

Then one day a man drove by and saw something besides an eyesore. He saw potential. With the existence of new technology, he wondered what treasures could be unearthed out of that castoff pile that everyone simply wanted gone. So he bought it. He remined that slag and came away with millions of dollars in "throwaway" gold.

Think of the slag in your life and the potential there is if you are willing to re-mine it. Go back and think of the lessons you learned, the experiences you garnered, the growth you enjoyed. If the earth beneath our feet is God's bank, then what are our lives to Him?

In God's economy, nothing is slag. Nothing is wasted. Every relationship we build is a teacher, every experience we have is a coach. In every scar there is a lesson. In every memory there is potential to make more memories.

Are you getting the point? You don't have to look back on your life with sorrow and regret. In the refining process, any experience that makes us wiser and molds us into something more workable for God is not wasted. A failed marriage, a lost business, a wrong choice—think of them as slag that simply makes the better part of us more visible.

But how exactly does this part of the process work? How can we take a sin, a mistake, sorrow, or suffering and turn it into something of value? The truth is, we can't. But God can. It's one of the things He does best. Romans 8:28 assures us, "And we know that all things work together for good to them that love God, to them who are called according to his purpose."

His purpose is to save us. If we love God (and we do!), then we are called to do everything we can to help Him save us. We let the Atonement of Christ refine the slag in our lives. We trust that in the end, nothing will be wasted. "Now the Spirit knoweth all things; nevertheless the Son of God suffereth according to the flesh that he might take upon him the sins of his people, that he might blot out their transgressions according to the power of his deliverance" (Alma 7:13).

The Atonement of Jesus Christ is available to each of us. His Atonement is infinite. It applies to you. It can clean, reclaim, and sanctify you. There's nothing you've thought or done or felt that falls outside the perimeters of the Atonement. That's what *infinite* means—total, complete, all, forever. President Boyd K. Packer teaches that none of our habits, transgressions, apostasies, addictions, rebellions, or crimes are beyond the promise of total forgiveness. That, he reminds us, is the promise of the Savior's Atonement (see "The Brilliant Morning of Forgiveness," *Ensign*, Nov. 1995, 20).

Repent

Repentance is like the man who saw something others did not: value in slag. When we fall to our knees, confess our sins, beg forgiveness, forsake our sins, and live better than we have before, our slag is not wasted. We become instruments in helping others who are thinking like I used to—that I'd wasted so much of my life, that the best was behind me, that I'd failed.

Repentance doesn't just recycle; it replaces. It takes what was rotten and makes it fresh, what was worn and makes it new, what was dead and breathes into it new life. How grateful we are that our Heavenly Father has given us the gift of repentance. And how sad it is if we do not recognize that each day is the time for us to make needed improvements: "But wo unto him that has the law given, yea, that has all the commandments of God, like unto us, and that transgresseth them, and that wasteth the days of his probation, for awful is his state!" (2 Ne. 9:27).

Three Examples of Hope for Me

What do the scriptures tell us about waste? Moses enjoyed a privileged life in the pharoah's palace—a Hebrew by birth but a prince by privilege—wanting for nothing while his fellow Hebrews were impoverished and enslaved. One day Moses witnessed one of his fellowmen being mistreated; he lost his temper and murdered the abuser. He broke what would become the sixth commandment he would one day carry down from Mount Sinai. He was forced to flee and ended up in a faraway land for forty years, forced to work by the sweat of his brow for the first time in his life.

Were those forty years wasted? Hardly. God took a man with a volatile temper, a man capable of manslaughter, a man who ran away, a man who struggled to communicate because his first language was Egyptian, not Hebrew, and who very well may have had a speech impediment on top of that. In essence, God saw in a flawed man someone capable of becoming a liberator, a lawgiver, and one of the greatest prophets and miracle-workers of all time. In those forty years, Moses became a husband, a father, and a shepherd. This was not wasted time but preparation time, for Moses had great things yet to do—starting with a burning bush.

Joseph, sold into slavery by his own brothers, ended up in the land of nonbelievers. He was falsely accused and sent to prison, where he stayed for a very long time, seemingly forgotten. But the Lord doesn't forget His children. Joseph stayed faithful and was blessed with the ability to interpret dreams—including Pharoah's dream, the interpretation of which became his ticket out of prison and his appointment as governor of all of Egypt. We never know where we'll end up as long as we are willing to endure injustice and remain faithful for a season or two or ten.

Saul was a devout Jew and a persecutor of the Christians. He was no innocent bystander at the stoning of Stephen. Then he made a trip to Damascus, where along the road his name changed to Paul and his life changed for eternity. What about all of those years he had worked so hard to destroy the gospel of Jesus Christ and to harm the faithful? Did God keep bringing up Paul's past, reminding him of the person he used to be? No. That is not what a loving God does. A loving God uses the slag from our past to make our future one of lessons learned. He turns our weaknesses into strengths and refines the slag—and even the solid impurities known as dross—from our lives. He keeps at it until we are pure and valuable. For even in a man as weak as Moses, there was tremendous strength; in a man as forsaken as Joseph, there was a leader; in a sinner as guilty as Saul, there was an apostle.

President James E. Faust tells us something of the process: "In the pain, the agony, and the heroic endeavors of life, we pass through a refiner's fire, and the insignificant and the unimportant in our lives can melt away like dross and make our faith bright, intact, and strong" ("Refined in Our Trials," *Ensign*, Feb. 2006).

What's in you? What is it going to take to make us all appreciate life more, the good and the bad?

Imagine

Imagine that you have been accused of a crime you did not commit. It doesn't matter; you've been found guilty, and you are sentenced to die. The execution is staged before an audience. You are asked to dig your own grave while the audience watches in amusement, for they are in on a little secret not privy to you. You're not really going to die. It's only a mock execution. Because you do not know that, every shovelful of dirt brings you closer to the end of your life. Every peal of laughter is torture from those who watch you. Then you are given your last meal and asked to speak your final words. A blindfold is tied around your eyes, and a cold gun barrel is pushed against your temple. You are about to die and you wait for it . . . *click.*

The laughter is like thunder. The blindfold comes off, and you're on your knees with dirt up your nose and blood in your mouth before you're informed of the joke.

What a horrible, ungodly thing to do. Yet it was not an uncommon occurrence in nineteenth-century Russia, where a writer named Fyodor Dostoevsky, who stood accused of political crimes, was put through this horrendous psychological trauma.

After that ordeal he was sentenced to four years of hard labor in Siberian work camps. Of his life he wrote, "When I look back on my past and think how much time I wasted on nothing, how much time has been lost in futilities, errors, laziness, incapacity to live; how little I appreciated it, how many times I sinned against my heart and soul—then my heart bleeds. Life is a gift, life is happiness, every minute can be an eternity of happiness!" (Joseph Frank, *Dostoevsky: The Years of Ordeal, 1850–1859* [Princeton, NJ: Princeton University Press, January 1984]).

Not Too Late

If you fear that you've wasted years of your life in the wrong job, hanging around the wrong people, doing the wrong things, God will gather those years and restore them to you. He'll take those experiences that the enemy meant for your harm and turn them around for your good. He'll make you stronger, wiser, and better off than you were before. He can launch you further into your destiny than before.

Be encouraged that you can give your slag to God and He will take it and make something of value from it. We worship a God who does not waste an experience, a hurt, a relationship, a dream, or even a crust of leftover bread.

CHAPTER FIVE

Wait for It

"Let us run with patience the race that is set before us, looking unto Jesus the author and finisher of our faith . . ." —Heb. 12:1–2

HE WAS ALMOST THERE. There were ten markers to the top of the mountain, and my son was at the eighth one when he fell to the ground and cried, "I give up!"

No matter how I bribed or threatened him, his six-year-old stubbornness won out. I collapsed on the ground next to him and said, "I'm not leaving you behind. If you give up, then I give up too."

He didn't give a second thought to my warped attempt at reverse psychology. So with our heads pillowed on the rocky terrain, the two of us lay on our backs looking up at a summer-blue sky.

An eagle soared high above us, like a black dot against all eternity. For a good minute we stayed put and watched the bird soar.

"What are you two doing?"

My eldest son had loped to the top of the mountain and was now barreling his way back down.

"He quit," I explained, jabbing a thumb in my young son's direction.

"It's too far and too hard," my little one whined.

"But you're almost there," my teenager said, hoisting his little brother up onto his shoulders and trudging back up the mountain. "I'll help you partway."

By the time I'd gotten on my feet and started upward I heard my eldest say to my youngest, "You have to go the rest of the way on your own. The finish is just around the bend."

And my little guy, renewed and encouraged, did just that. He actually ran the distance from marker nine to the finish at marker ten.

I've hiked that trail many times since then, and every time I approach marker eight it occurs to me that just when we are at our most weary and weakest and we most want to give up, help comes from above. I'm reminded that though we are all on the same journey our legs are different lengths and our abilities vary. I think that sometimes it's good to stop and rest. If I had kept my eyes to the ground and my feet steady, I would have missed seeing that eagle soar. The Lord will walk with us. He will come to our aid. He will even carry us partway, but in the end, we have to do our part.

Christ, on the cross, was left to finish on His own.

Though God gave Noah inspiration and instruction on how to build an ark, Noah himself had to pick up a hammer and a saw.

The pioneers were promised safety in a land where they could worship freely. But those faithful men, women, and children had to put one foot in front of the other and trek the thirteen hundred miles to claim it.

Henry David Thoreau penned, "All endeavor calls for the ability to tramp the last mile, shape the last plan, endure the last hours toil. The fight to the finish spirit is the one . . . characteristic we must posses if we are to face the future as finishers" (Sandra Harbert Petrulionis, ed., *Thoreau in His Own Time: A Biographical Chronicle of His Life* [Iowa City, IA: University of Iowa Press, 2012]).

Refining our commitment, then, requires that we join forces with the Lord and make certain we complete our leg of the journey, no matter how treacherous, no matter how long.

Tick-Tock

After the slag phase in the refinery comes a cooling-off period when all that happens is waiting. This has to occur if the gold is going to be separated from the impurities, yet it appears as if nothing is happening.

Tick. Tock. Tick. Tock. Tick. Tock.

How often do we feel like we are in one of those "waiting" stages?

To an outsider it may appear as if no change is occurring. It may even seem that way to us. But to a God who knows us and works His miracles from the inside out, the refining process is progressing perfectly.

Think about Abraham. All his adult life he'd longed for a son. God promised him one. He trusted God's word no matter how foolish he appeared to his community and even to his aging wife. He longed for a boy to bear his name and likeness, to carry on the work to which Abraham had given his life. This great man's faith is exemplary.

Someone raised the question: Did Abraham wait so patiently and obediently because he loved God or because he so desperately wanted a son? An important part of the refining process, especially during the waiting phase, is to examine our motives.

In one of my psychology classes the professor taught that we set goals for one of two reasons: to achieve success or to avoid failure. A bit of both may exist in the same person, and two people may strive toward the same goal for very different reasons. Another professor touted that by human nature, we are motivated by either wanting to find pleasure or to avoid pain. Albert Einstein, a self-proclaimed atheist, said, "Feeling and longing are the motive forces behind all human endeavor and human creations" (Albrecht Folsing and Ewald Osers, *Albert Einstein: A Biography* [New York: Penguin Books, 1998], 44).

As Latter-day Saints, part of our refining process, especially during the "waiting" period, is examining our motives and asking ourselves why we do the things we do. We know we are children of a Father who has endowed us with His power and His love, so our expectations are high. Are we obedient to His commandments because we want the blessings or because we love the Lord? Do we keep our covenants out of fear or love—or maybe a bit of both? There are times when God is more of a means to an end than *the* means and the end.

We are faithful paying our tithing because we hope for monetary recompense. We serve a mission because we want the recognition. Why do we go to church, attend the temple, or accept callings? I'll be honest—some Sundays I feel like I'm barely going through the motions. I feel better when I remind myself that I attend church because I love the Lord. If I do it because I feel pressured, I don't receive the same portion of the Spirit. Obligation, guilt, fear, pride, and every impure motive has to be separated from the golden motive that outweighs the slag: the love of God. Jesus said He did "always those things" that pleased God (John 8:29).

I can't say my motive is always pure, but I can say that I'm working toward that end. I want a pure heart. I want to serve because I love the Lord. Knowing that the Lord is patient with me tells me that I should be patient with myself. President Ezra Taft Benson taught that we can best examine our motives by asking ourselves if our decision is based on charity or on personal gain (see Ezra Taft Benson, *Teachings of Ezra Taft Benson* [Salt Lake City: Deseret Book Company, 1998], 369).

When we have a decision to make, we can ask ourselves if our motives are born of charity or some type of personal gain. Is it really that simple? Let's take a look at the life of Abraham, who must have felt forever stuck in the "waiting period."

Abraham was born in the land of Ur, where his own father, Tehran, worshipped idols. History suggests that Tehran carved the idols, which means Abraham saw his father create gods from wood or stone. Then Abraham saw people praying before those very idols. He saw them lay sacrifices at the feet of gods Abraham knew were nothing more than lumps of organic material.

This made no sense to Abraham. He sought "for mine appointment unto the Priesthood" (Abr. 1:4.) He said that he desired great knowledge, and to be "a greater follower of righteousness" (Abr. 1:2).

The conditions around him grew so vile that Abraham suffered a mock execution of his own. He was bound and laid on an altar to be sacrificed before a god crafted from the hand of man. Abraham prayed with urgent faith, and at the last moment an angel delivered him (see Abr. 1:12–15).

He left the land of idolatry and continued to be prayerful and faithful. He married Sarah and desired with all of his heart to become a father. Though he was a mighty prophet who knew that God heard and answered prayers, the burning desire in his heart to have a son seemed to be a prayer left unanswered. After further refining of his already-refined faith, the Spirit of God made Abraham a promise: Abraham would have a son—not just any son but one who would grant him a posterity whose numbers would outnumber the stars in the sky and the sands of the sea. Abraham believed. He waited. And waited. And waited.

Year followed year. Sarah grew older until it was clear that, physically, her childbearing years were past. Still Abraham waited. Sarah must have felt an entire spectrum of emotions as she saw her husband's faith challenged while he suffered. She didn't want to wait on the Lord another minute, so she did what we're all tempted to do when things don't move as fast as we'd like—she got ahead of the Lord and took it upon herself to solve the problem. The scriptures are sparse in detail, but Sarah gave her servant to Abraham so that he could have the son he had ached for all of his life.

We all know how that worked out.

Fourteen long, long years passed while Sarah witnessed for herself what happens when we try to outrun the Lord. Finally, as promised, her barren, almost century-old womb brought forth the son that Abraham had waited for most of his life.

Can you imagine the love Abraham felt for Isaac? Can you picture the time spent between Abraham and Isaac as Abraham groomed Isaac to be the one to carry on the work of God? How devoted they must have been to each other! How Abraham must have loved God for finally granting him the promised son.

But then the unthinkable happened. The very God who had given Isaac wanted him back. "Take now thy son, thine only son Isaac, whom thou lovest, and get thee into the land of Moriah; and offer him there for a burnt offering upon one of the mountains which I will tell thee of" (Gen. 22:2).

Can you feel the refiner's flames burn hotter than ever? Can you imagine what Abraham must have felt as he did what was required of him? Note that he rose up "early" and traveled for three days, all the while knowing what was coming. And still he journeyed on.

Why would a loving God require such a sacrifice from a man who had already proven his obedience time and time again? Wasn't Abraham's faith already refined to 24-karat gold?

He tells the servants who had come with them, "Abide ye here with the ass; and I and the lad will go yonder and worship, and come again to you" (Gen. 22:5).

Stop! Reread that passage. Abraham is telling his servants that after he and Isaac worship *they* ("I and the lad") will return.

I don't think for a moment that Abraham believed God would not require Isaac. I don't think for a moment that Abraham doubted God. But Abraham himself had once been laid on the altar and had been delivered by the hand of God. Would He not do the same for Isaac?

Talk about using our past—especially the negative experiences—as slag that can be refined into something useful.

I believe with all of my heart that Abraham had so much faith in a loving Lord that three options were possible: One, Isaac would be spared as Abraham had been spared. Two, even if Isaac died, God would be able to restore him to life. And three, Abraham would return with a corpse and know that he had given his all to the God who requires nothing less of us.

No matter. Abraham was headed to the altar.

He proved obedient in the face of a sacrifice I can't begin to fathom. Before that he'd been through a lifetime of waiting, of refining. There was no question about his allegiance. God was not a means to an end, the way to get something he wanted. God was what Abraham wanted, and he proved it.

How long are you and I willing to wait on the Lord?

How Long?

I have a friend who is forty-four years old. She has been married to the love of her life since she was nineteen. All she's ever wanted is to be a wife and a mother. As newlyweds they bought a crib before they bought pots and pans. By twenty-two, my friend was saying, "Some dreams just take longer to come true." So she went to college and became a pediatric nurse. By thirty, she'd become a full-fledged pediatrician.

Countless prayers have been offered, blessings given in faith, covenants honored.

No doctor has been able to determine why she and her husband cannot conceive. "We'll adopt," she announced at her thirty-third birthday party. And they put in the papers and waited. And waited some more. A little girl was promised them, but the birth father rescinded the offer three weeks before the baby was born.

Years later an adoption from a third-world country was arranged, papers were signed, and money paid. We were so confident this time around that we threw her a surprise baby shower. We were hauling gifts to her car when the telephone call came with the horrible news that the baby had been delivered early and stillborn.

"Some dreams," my friend now says, "never come true."

Another friend of mine suffered abuse when she was a young girl at the hands of someone who should have been a mentor and protector. She struggled to feel worthy of any blessing and barely dared hope to become a wife. Eventually she married in the temple, and nothing meant more to her than becoming a mother.

She works as a nurse at the same hospital that employs my pediatrician friend. When the doctors told her that it was unlikely she'd ever be able to have children, she asked her husband for a blessing. In it she was promised that from her body children would be born and raised in her loving care.

A year passed. Then five. Then ten. After selling their home and moving into an apartment so they could afford fertility treatments, after so many heartbreaking disappointments, a call came on Christmas Eve from a jolly doctor who announced, "You're pregnant with twins!"

It wasn't an easy pregnancy. We all held our breath for nine months, but today those little wonders are growing strong and healthy.

Why was one woman allowed to become a mother and the other denied that honor? I don't have the answer, but I know God does.

"It's just not fair," someone said.

We were never promised that life would be fair. Or easy. We *were* promised the same comfort God promised Moses: "Be strong and of a good courage, fear not, nor be afraid of them: for the Lord thy God, he it is that doth go with thee; he will not fail thee, nor forsake thee" (Deut. 31:6). We were promised that God would be with us.

Part of the refining process is to suffer loss and disappointment. All human beings go through it—some kicking and screaming, some giving up, and some adapting in faith, managing to maintain a positive perspective and an even balance.

True disciples of Christ reach to touch the edge of his garment for healing and strength when life batters us about or, worse, when it all stands still and we don't seem to make any progress at all. Usually it is only after the waiting period is over that we can look back and see that the Lord used disappointment to open a different door than the one on which we were pounding (see Matt. 7:7).

Scar Stories

The prophet Isaiah said, "And therefore will the Lord wait, that he may be gracious unto you, and therefore will he be exalted, that he may have mercy upon you" (Isa. 30:18).

I once conducted a yearlong seminar program on how to write your family history, to tell the story that only you can tell. During that process I looked down at a nasty scar on my thumb; looking at that scar reminded me of the burn that had caused it. I was prompted to consider how interesting our life stories would be if we told them scar by scar.

I have several scars from where I conquered cancer. I have a doozy of a scar on my hand where a camel attempted to rid me of my thumb. I have scars from giving birth and scars from falling hard while hiking and biking and boating. Besides the camel that took a chunk out of me, little scars remind me that I've been bitten by a goose, a snake, a kangaroo, a monkey, a rabbit, a dog, a cat, a skunk, a cow, and a few horses. I used to work for a veterinarian who treated large animals, which accounts for a few of those scars. Obviously, I love animals more than they love me.

When I gave "the scar challenge" to the seminar attendees, one man showed a scar where he'd been stabbed in the back. A Vietnam veteran talked of hidden scars from bullet wounds and bad memories. A woman showed us a scar she'd received when she grabbed the handle of a hot pan. A teenager pointed to a scar on his forehead where he'd banged into a wall while sleepwalking. It became clear: We are all scarred.

Think about your own scars and the stories they tell. Now think of how long they took to heal and all that you learned from the waiting. There is not a lot we can do to expedite the healing process. We can slow it down by not taking care of our wounds and letting them get infected, but the healing process is like all of life's processes: It takes time and patience.

Who Knew

The apostle Paul knew about waiting and patience. Think of how he must have felt trapped in the underground dungeons of prisons while there was so much work to do in building the Lord's new kingdom on earth. I would have been frustrated like Martha in the kitchen, but Paul's writings tell us his mind was in a more peaceful, focused state. "Let us run with patience the race that is set before us," he admonished (Heb. 12:1).

How can you run a race with patience? You've got to run a race fast and furiously and get to the finish line first. Isn't that the purpose of a race? Not if you're running against yourself, and that's who we are all running against—ourselves.

King Benjamin would have listed patience as one of the most "needful" things in the refining process. He taught that patience is among the most important attributes we can claim (see Mosiah 3:19). The Prophet Joseph Smith, like Moses, yearned to get to the promised land, where his people could worship without persecution. Neither one of them made it. But Joseph made it far beyond the Utah Territory. Patience in his life played a refining role in preparing him for "a more exceeding and eternal weight of glory" (D&C 63:66).

There are times and seasons when it is easier to exhibit patience. Children can sit still longer if they know there's a treat waiting at the end of five minutes. Impatience, on the other hand, opens the oven door before the cake is baked, causing it to fall in the middle. Impatience robs us of the lessons that patience wants and needs to teach us. Sometimes running our race with patience means staying still and waiting—waiting for our slag to rise to the top and the gold in our souls to outweigh it.

CHAPTER SIX

Acid Baths

"Thou knowest the greatness of God; and he shall consecrate thine afflictions for thy gain." —2 Ne. 2:2

IMAGINE THAT YOU'RE STANDING AT the gates of a great stadium unlike any stadium you've known, anxious to enter the game that is being played on the field. It's the game of life. The price of admission comes with a ticket labeled *adversity*. If you want to enter the arena you have to agree to suffer pain, humiliation, rejection, stress, injury, disappointment, catastrophic loss, and various other unpleasant surprises.

We were all at those gates. We agreed to the cost. We entered the game.

Now that we're here and have the scars to prove it, do we want things differently? One weekend I watched my son race in a major track meet; as I waited for him, I watched the hurdlers. How they could do what they did amazed me. I find it difficult to jump over the toys left on the floor in my house. But there they were, high school kids taking on a sixty-meter indoor race over five hurdles.

Bang! The gun went off and so did the hurdlers. They seemed to be in exact sync, legs and bodies pumping and jumping. I must have watched twenty heats as the competition became tighter, the timing within hundredths of a second.

Then came the champion—a boy with the fastest record in the state. He looked confident and absolutely ready. I held my breath as I watched them race toward the first hurdle.

Then it happened—something I had not witnessed in twenty heats. On the first hurdle the champ caught his shoe and down he went, face first. He landed so hard I thought he might have broken his nose. It must have stunned him, because by the time he managed to get back on his feet the race was over.

Not for him.

That boy, dazed as he was, finished his race. He set the fallen hurdle back up, pedaled backward, and cleared all five hurdles. I don't know that I've ever cheered that hard.

"Too bad he lost," someone next to me said.

"He didn't lose," I replied.

The man rolled his eyes and pointed to the clock.

Some victories cannot be timed. Some victories cannot be seen. Some victories will never be rewarded on earth but will be celebrated only on the other side of eternity.

Acid and Agitation

I hated to see that boy fall. But would we really want a life without hurdles that crash to the ground with our dreams? How could there be true champions then? If the pioneers had not suffered when crossing the plains, would we herald them as Saints? Intense pressure is needed to make a diamond from coal; intense heat is required to separate gold from rock. So what is required to produce the best in us?

After we patiently wait to see what happens in the refining process, after the slag and the good stuff are divided, the refining process continues so that even the smallest particles of gold get separated. There's more heat and agitation followed by a not-so-pleasant bath in something called aqua-regia, which is a combination of nitric acid and hydrochloric acid. Now doesn't that sound like a fun Friday night?

Take heart in knowing that the heat has can't be turned up too high, otherwise the aqua-regia boils and produces brown fumes that waste acid and obscure the end of the solvent action. The reaction actually slows down at this stage because of the amount of fine sludge that tends to restrict the contact between aqua-regia and undissolved gold. Considerable agitation and stirring are required to keep the reaction going. Think of agitation as adversity and acid as . . . well, more adversity, the kind that burns sin from our souls and doubt from our hearts—the kind that destroys the impurities within us.

Who wants to take an acid bath? Not me.

I don't suppose Peter was in the mood for one either. Yet, isn't that exactly what he got when the waves took him under?

Right after Jesus had fed the five thousand with miracle fish and bread, He instructed His disciples to board a small ship and cross the Sea of Galilee. He wanted to stay behind to bid good-bye to the multitude and spend some time in personal prayer. We cannot miss the fact that Jesus was going through His own painful refiner's fire: He'd just lost His beloved cousin John, the one who'd baptized Him, to the barbaric beheading ordered by Herod. Jesus wanted to be alone to pray. But He looked out and saw that His disciples were in a ship being tossed about by a storm that had risen on the sea. Jesus had a choice. He could stay and feel sad, or He could get up and go help His friends. Oft times, our refinement comes in making simple decisions.

The night was dark and windy. The waves were breaking hard and the ship was being batted back and forth. Fear gripped the disciples. Add to the storm their fear when they peered out through the pelting water to see what they took to be a spirit walking toward them. Jesus never wants to "scare" us, so He announced His identity. Peter, among others, was skeptical. "Lord, if it be thou, bid me come unto thee on the water." And Jesus responded, "Come" (Matt. 14:28–29).

Give Peter credit. At least he got out of the ship. He had faith enough to join the Master's miracle. His feet stayed atop the waves for a time. But then Peter did what we all tend to do when the storms of life attack us: He took his eyes off Jesus and focused on the power of the storm. Immediately his faith in Christ and in himself wanted, and he began to sink. The sea was ready to swallow Peter when he cried, "Lord, save me" (Matt. 14:30).

Jesus saved him. He didn't wait. He stretched forth His hand *immediately*.

Talk about an acid bath! Peter went down just like that hurdler at the track meet. Our refinement isn't all about the falling; it's about the rising. The young hurdler proved himself a true champ by racing again, though he had no shot of winning. Peter proved he still had faith in Christ by crying out to Him when his faith was as troubled as the waves on the sea.

Christ asks, "wherefore didst thou doubt?" (Matt. 14:31). The Greek word for doubt—*distazo*—does not imply skepticism, but vacillation. What happens when we vacillate during an acid bath? We splash around; we get dipped and dipped again. But when we trust in the Lord, we find a way to conquer the fear and endure the pain, and we come out purer than we were. That's the promise the Refiner makes. And He always, always keeps His promises.

Understanding Adversity

1. Adversity is the price of admission. Adversity is going to come your way. Pain and death are inevitable. To try to avoid them is to avoid life. But suffering is not mandatory—you can know pain without knowing suffering.

2. Adversity defines abundance. I didn't realize how blessed I was to live in the United States until I visited third-world countries. We need doubt to appreciate faith, loneliness to appreciate love, winter to appreciate spring.

3. Adversity does not punish. It polishes—if we allow it. Sometimes what we see as adversity is really a chance for us to grow.

As human beings, we tend to be mentally complacent, physically comfortable, and spiritually comatose. If we aren't forced to do so, we don't like to move. When a mother eagle believes her eaglets are ready to take flight, she begins to disassemble the nest. For those babies who cling and claw to stay, she gives the necessary nudge. How will we ever know we can fly if we aren't nudged off the edge?

4. One dose of adversity is easier to wrestle. Dwelling on the pain of the past resurrects it. Worrying about the future invites it. Know this: An acid bath is meant to separate the precious metal, not dissolve it. In fact, it *won't* dissolve it, though it probably feels that way to the gold. With the additive of faith, the acid bath of adversity dissolves everything until all that is left is who we actually are.

5. Gratitude softens the blow of adversity. A refiner put a piece of gold iron in my hand. I saw tiny specks and veins of glitter within the rock. "Why do you think God hides what is most valuable and beautiful in something so hard?" he asked. "Why does He bury it so deep within the rock?"

"I don't know."

"So we will appreciate it."

When we have to go through a great deal to get what we want, we appreciate it more. When we are aware and grateful, adversity loses its punch. Don't worry so much about what you don't have—just focus on the moment and on your blessings and know that God will be with you through the trials of your faith if you do as Peter did and call out for help.

A Big Fat Lie

I received a letter during the most painful time of my divorce from someone I thought knew me. In essence it told me that if I had more faith, this trial would not have come upon me. Later, when I was laid up in the hospital with a broken leg from an accident, another person told me that if I'd had more faith, the bus on which I was riding would not have blown a tire. If I'd had more faith, lightning would not have struck my house. My child would not be sick. My neighbor's dog would not have violated my flower garden.

Really? A friend of mine, a dear soul who has lived with a faithful husband, five obedient children, and an inheritance that requires a special bank vault, sat on my sofa. I knew she was a woman of profound faith, so I told her what I'd been hearing and asked her what she thought. Why had I had been born to parents who did not believe? Why did my father die when I was a toddler? Why was my mother an alcoholic? Why had I been abused at the hands of people in power and authority over me—people who should have been protecting me? Why had those I believed in broken their vows and covenants, leaving me and my children to suffer? The list went on.

"Are you feeling sorry for yourself?" she asked.

"Yes, a bit."

She looked at me sincerely and said, "I think it's because the Lord favors some of His children over others. I hate to admit it, but perhaps you are being punished for your lack of faith. Perhaps you weren't as valiant in the pre-existence and that's why you have the trials you have."

I swallowed her answer hook, line, and sinker. It was like swallowing a barbed hook. And because I swallowed it, I floundered for a long time, a dying fish flapping on the banks of the river. I looked at others and saw their seemingly easy lives and made the kind of comparisons none of us should ever make. I judged them and I judged myself. I kept coming back to my friend's idea that the Lord did not favor my children, that my lack of faith was inviting trials for me. I prayed for more faith. I acted like someone starved for a spiritual meal. I blamed and berated myself, and I felt with all of my heart that no matter how hard I tried, I still came up short in the eyes of the Lord.

What my friend told me is false doctrine according to the Prophet Joseph Smith. His teachings tell us that it's wrong and false to believe that we Saints will manage to escape the judgments—like sickness, loss, disease, pestilence, war, and so on—that accompany the last days. My friend was wrong because it is not a correct principle to judge another's faith and to say that adversities are due to transgression (Joseph Fielding Smith, Jr., comp., *Teachings of the Prophet Joseph Smith* [Salt Lake City: Deseret Book Company], 162).

Then I met a Kenyan woman who stood a head taller than me. Her legs were long and her muscles lean. She grinned at me with a smile as wide as the Rift Valley. "I am a jumper," she said.

That she was. Her name was Gift, and Gift's long jump record registered nearly fourteen meters. In a contest of fun and a lot of laughter, I challenged her nearly six-foot frame of lean muscle mass to my five-and-a-half-foot frame of just plain mass. She went flying and planted her heels a mile away in the soft red dirt. My long jump registered about the length of my shoe.

We laughed and hugged, and I remembered a sermon I'd attended in which the minister called a long-jumper out of the audience. The man was an Olympic athlete. Then the minister beckoned another audience member up, a fellow born the same year as the athlete. They stood toe-to-toe on the podium, looking as mismatched as Gift and I must have appeared. The minister laid down a piece of bright yellow tape, obviously the goal marker.

"Is it fair of me to require that these two individuals jump the same distance?" he asked.

Hands went up and people cried out, "No, it's not fair. One is more qualified and able to jump farther."

"You're right," said the minister. But he still asked the two men to jump as far as they could from the starting mark to the finish line of yellow tape. The first jumper, an accountant who sat at a desk eight hours each day, jumped far, but nowhere near the marker. When it was his turn, the athlete seemed to spring not only toward the goal line but beyond it.

"What's the point?" the minister asked.

"You're showing that we are all different," someone suggested. "Our skill levels and abilities are not equal."

Then the minister lined the two men up again. "Now, suppose I place these two men at the edge of the Grand Canyon in Arizona and ask them to jump to the other side."

The audience went silent until someone finally replied, "It would not matter that one man could out-jump the other. The end result would be that both men would fall far short. Both men would surely die."

The minister grinned. "That is the point! We all fall short of the mark, no matter how good we are, no matter how many commandments we can check off. That's where Jesus Christ has to come in and manage us all the way across. *Only* He can make up the difference because we all fall short."

Some of us despise adversity. We think of how much better our life would be if we could just have an obstacle-free course. The funny thing about adversity is that without it, we simply don't grow. It's the process of overcoming adversity that brings out the best in us—that challenges us and allows us to become stronger.

I go to the gym. I watch bodybuilders lift weights. I see them get stronger and their muscles get bigger. It's the opposition from the weight against the strength of their muscles that causes the muscles to grow. I see them begin with small amounts of weight and progress until they can lift twice, three times, five times their first amount. We need opposition in order to gain strength. It's the way the Lord designed our bodies and our spirits.

Acid Burns

Acid is meant to clean and dissolve what is corroded or unwanted. It burns. It hurts. It can scar or even kill if not handled with proper care. I once knocked myself almost unconscious trying to clean the bathtub with muriatic acid. I didn't know what I was doing but the Lord knows exactly what He is doing, and we cannot allow ourselves to forget that.

I realize that when life is painful it's not likely that you're going to stop and remind yourself, "Oh, this acid bath I'm in is for my own good. When it's over I'll be cleaner and more refined than I was. The Lord's in charge; I'm not."

When we repent we essentially ask for an acid bath. We want the Lord to remove our sins completely. We want to be made sparkling new. So as you face adversity on your journey through life, face it head on. Revel in the chance to prove yourself and enjoy the challenge much the same way a professional athlete enjoys a strenuous workout.

After I've lifted weights one day, I wake up the next day in pain. It happens every time because my muscles are being torn and challenged and made stronger. It's a good kind of pain.

But pain is still pain, and it hurts.

My friend's judgment of me caused pain. Her words hurt, but over time and with an understanding of adversity, I realized that her words were just that: words. There is no reference in all of scripture, ancient or modern, that says God punishes those who struggle to do their best. In fact, when Peter's faith vacillated, the Lord's hand went out *immediately* to help him.

Job saw the big picture that would benefit us all. A man of righteousness, he was very blessed, and then he was put through a refiner's fire hotter than anything I can imagine. His question is a defining one: "Shall we indeed accept good from God, and shall we not accept adversity?" (Job 2:10).

We do that. We take the good things in life with little more than "Thanks, Heavenly Father." But when adversity comes, our prayers fail to even mention gratitude.

For his awareness of this and for his unwavering faith, Job was restored and rewarded beyond all that he'd lost. Joseph Smith was able to establish Nauvoo and its temple only *after* he'd suffered in Liberty Jail, paying a price I can only imagine. Spencer W. Kimball became prophet and spokesman for God *only* after he had suffered the loss of one vocal cord and half the other. He could bear testimony of his "silent, sleepless night" only *after* he had suffered through it.

How could my thinking have been so skewed? Heavenly Father does not spare anyone from adversity, and He doesn't punish us with it. I had some repenting to do. I'd given more merit to someone else's opinion than to the Lord's word: My faith would increase only *after* the trial of my faith (see Ether 12:6). Think about that: to have our faith strengthened, it must be tried.

As always, Jesus set the standard: "Though he were a Son, yet learned he obedience by the things which he suffered" (Heb. 5:8).

"And he shall go forth, suffering pains and afflictions and temptations of every kind; and this that the word might be fulfilled which saith he will take upon him the pains and the sicknesses of his people.

"And he will take upon him death, that he may loose the bands of death which bind his people; and he will take upon him their infirmities, that his bowels may be filled with mercy, according to the flesh, that he may know according to the flesh how to succor his people according to their infirmities" (Alma 7:11–12).

If Jesus and Joseph and Job were not spared, why would I be spared? I wouldn't be, and I haven't been. My trials continue. I am in need of prolonged and sustained refinement. The Lord is in charge, and He has my best interest at heart because He knows me.

Faith in the Refiner

In the previous chapter we discussed how nothing is wasted in the Lord's economy. Still, we hurt. When we lose something there is pain. It might not be lost to the Lord, but to us it doesn't feel that way. When we lose a job we suffer. When our health fails we suffer. When a loved one dies, that loss seems eternal. That yearning to ask "How could this happen?" is more painful when it happens to someone we love, especially to someone who seems blameless.

My passion is to help God's children, especially His little ones. After the earthquakes in Haiti I saw suffering like I've never witnessed, especially among the innocent children. I've been privileged to work with the children of the world and the children in my own home. It breaks my heart to see them suffer because they are innocent, yet even they are not spared.

I know a man whose son was not spared tremendous suffering. His son had come to him with a shattered heart following the death of his wife and unborn child. "Father, help me understand. I have done what was asked of me. In high school, I stayed morally clean when my peers were immoral. I did not drink. I did not smoke. I didn't even swear. I served an honorable mission. I married in the temple. We did not wait to start our family. Now it seems I'm being punished in the worst imaginable way. Why, Father, why?"

This young man's father sobbed as he testified of the experience. "I could only hold my son in my arms and tell him that I had no answer. Only God could answer why."

My testimony to you today is the same as that father's testimony. I have no answer to so many of life's "whys." But I do know that the price of admission into this life was a willingness to face adversity, to go through the process of refinement. It's an ongoing process that involves incalculable pain and a testing of our faith and a willingness to obey.

To know our Refiner we must believe his words: "I . . . will try them as gold is tried: they shall call on my name, and I will hear them: I will say, It is my people: and they shall say, The Lord is my God" (Zech. 13:9).

Isn't that the real goal—to know God?

Acid burns away the impurities from gold. Adversity burns away the impurities from our lives. It's that painful. It's that practical. And it's that necessary. It's the price of admission to the big event we call life.

CHAPTER SEVEN

Who We Really Are

"What manner of men ought ye to be?
Verily I say unto you, even as I am."
—3 Ne. 27:27

WHEN YOU ARE ALL ALONE, are you in good company?

Are you the person you want to be? If you were in complete charge of your own refinement, what changes would you make to yourself? My personal list goes on and on. I'd change just about everything: whittle away some places, pad other places, and polish the whole kit and caboodle. I want to become a "new creature," as Paul put it, but not just any new creature—a new creature in Christ with the promise that old things are passed away and all things are become new (see 2 Cor. 5:17).

In essence, we do have the opportunity to remake ourselves—to reshape our lives and to rid the impurities from our minds, our hearts, and our bodies. The Refiner is Jesus Christ, and His refinery is the Atonement. The Atonement is a no-fail program that guarantees refinishing and refining if followed with faith and obedience. It's the only way I know to take something that is broken beyond repair and make it whole and new again.

We've addressed the stages of refinement: recognizing and desiring to change, assembling the right equipment, feeling the heat, realizing nothing is wasted in the Lord's economy, exercising faithful patience, and being willing to suffer the pain of acid refinement.

Now we've reached the stage in the process when all of our hard work begins to take shape. It's an exciting, complicated venture that requires skill and deliberate care.

It begins with a good washing. The caustic acid used earlier is neutralized with a pH-reducing uric acid. This draws out even the tiniest particles of gold. Then comes a slue of other additives and reactions. Finally there's a filtering so that none of the gold is lost— only the obstinate impurities are separated.

But it's not over yet. An additional melting occurs, and the gold is shaped and molded, usually into coins or bullion bars. If the mold is not warm and dry, the gold can become discolored or moisture can cause it to erupt. You do not ever want molten gold on your bare skin. Trust me on that one.

The Real Deal

I call this stage the real deal. It's all I've ever really wanted to be: genuine. I haven't always been and I won't always be, but it's what I want to be. I was in a meeting where testimonies were being shared and a woman started by saying, "I want to testify to you that Thomas S. Monson is the real deal. When he talks about visiting and blessing the sick, he is telling the truth. He used to live in our ward, and when he heard that my daughter had been stricken with a horrible disease that made her bones break when she attempted to stand or move, he went out of his way to come and bless her. That was thirty years ago. Today my daughter is here."

That daughter, a grown, healthy woman with a baby in her arms, stood up and bore her own testimony that Thomas S. Monson was not only a prophet of God, but a man of his word.

Thomas S. Monson says he is a prophet of God. He is. Jesus claims He is the Son of God. He is. Am I who I say I am? Are you? We take upon ourselves His holy name and call ourselves Christians, even Saints. A Christian is one who believes in Jesus Christ and His teachings. A Saint is an exceptionally holy person. The Latin word *sanctus* means "a holy one." So if we are Christian Saints, we've got a lot—A LOT—to live up to.

We've also got the ways and the means to do it—to become anything and anyone we desire. Please don't be discouraged; be encouraged. No matter who you are, no matter where you are, you have the potential to change, to be refined—"knock, and it shall be opened unto you" (3 Ne. 14:7). Imagine knocking on the Savior's door and asking, "Refine me, please. Make of me the person I am meant to be, the person I am capable of becoming."

Studying this process has taught me this: The Lord has a specific pattern and way of doing things. When we attempt to change on our own it doesn't work. When we rely on a way to do it without Him, it doesn't work. The one who has known us longest and best and who loves us most knows how to make us into the best version of ourselves we can be. He knows how to make us become more Christlike.

Only Way Out

The only way out is through. Joseph Smith had to go through months of suffering in Liberty Jail. Jesus Christ had to go through the agony of Gethsemane and the suffering on the cross before He could finally say, "It is finished." We go through cancer treatment, through a divorce, through a dark tunnel to get to the other side where the light shines again.

Is there something you are avoiding, something you are running away from? I asked myself this question and was led to this scripture: "O then despise not, and wonder not, but hearken unto the words of the Lord, and ask the Father in the name of Jesus for what things soever ye shall stand in need. Doubt not, but be believing, and begin as in times of old, and come unto the Lord with all your heart, and work out your own salvation with fear and trembling before him" (Morm. 9:27).

Despise not: The Lord reproves us because He loves us. He refines us because He wants us to have all that He has and to become like Him. Trust that He loves you—and if He is telling you to do something, do it knowing that it will work out in your best interest. There was a time when I went before the Lord asking how I could bring my family closer together. I was told to cook and clean more. Seriously. I hated that answer. I wanted the Spirit to whisper something like, "Take the kids to Disneyland." Nope. Cook and clean.

Wonder not: Don't go through life saying, "I wonder why I feel this way." Figure it out through the Spirit and take action. Once I received the prompting to cook and clean, I did those things. We set up chores and made a regular appointment for family dinners. Years have passed since that experience, and I testify to you that it worked.

Sister Margaret McConkie Pope, my Book of Mormon instructor at BYU, told our class, "I set the Sunday dinner table with my best dishes and make it very special when company is *not* coming. I want my family to know they are the most important people in my life."

It's a little trick that has worked wonders in our family, though I despised the advice at first and wondered why I'd ever get such an answer.

Hearken: We shouldn't simply listen and give attention to what is being said but we should inquire and seek information. The Lord wants to be in continual communication with us.

Ask: What do you need to make your life better? Ask the Lord. He wants us to ask Him (see 3 Ne. 14:7). I don't ask because I don't feel worthy. I don't ask because I think I have to do it on my own. I don't ask, and I don't receive. It's that simple and that sad. No matter what the matter, if it matters to you—ask.

Doubt not but be believing: That's easier said than done. One way to cease our doubts and increase our believing power is to remember what the Lord has already done for us. Count your blessings and know that He is still there, standing ready to help.

Begin: Stop procrastinating. I promise you the very second you commit yourself to the Lord's care, the moment you step out of the boat, the moment you stand to testify, the morning you put on your running shoes to get back into shape, every angel heaven can spare will be at your side to see you succeed.

Come unto the Lord with all your heart: Don't give Him a portion—give Him the full measure. Give all your heart, and know He'll give the same in return. Radical change requires radical action. Offer God only a bit of your heart if you want only a bit of His help.

Work out your own salvation with fear and trembling before Him: You are partners with the Lord. He never fails to do His part when we do ours—but it is a partnership, and the Lord will never force us to change because that would violate our agency.

The Lord's Way

The Lord is a god of order. If I want to refine gold from ore, I have to follow precise steps. They can't be skipped or taken out of order. God created the ore. He put the gold inside the ore. He put gold inside of you and me, too. He knows precisely how to get the best out of us.

His pattern is straightforward: "Line upon line, precept upon precept, here a little and there a little; and blessed are those who hearken unto my precepts" (2 Ne. 28:30).

Just as in the refining process, steps must be taken and order must be followed. The Lord has a pattern for doing things, and if we want to know if we are hearing from the Lord, we must learn to recognize and understand that pattern. To be like Him we must act like Him. "Come, follow me" (Luke 18:22).

Yes, the Lord answered Joseph Smith's prayer with one of the greatest revelations of all time. He put Jonah in the acidic belly of a whale to teach him a lesson. He put Alma the Younger in a coma and made a donkey reprimand Balaam. Obviously, the Lord can and does work fast and big from time to time. But for the most part, His supernatural ways are subtle and slow.

President Boyd K. Packer said that in his experience, the powerful, impressive spiritual experiences don't happen to us very often (see *That All May be Edified* [Salt Lake City: Bookcraft, 1982], 337).

Sometimes when I am stuck and don't know what to do, I stay put. I don't move. Guess what? Not much happens. Oh, there are times when I feel an impression or hear a whisper. Mostly, though, nothing happens until I move. Sometimes that's all I hear: "Do something!" This seems to be in direct contrast to our chapter on waiting patiently, but it is not. We wait when the waiting period arrives. When it's time for doing, we no longer just wait around.

To get the plates of brass, Lehi's sons had to make several attempts and had to come up with their own methods. To build a family transport ship, Nephi received instruction from "time to time" (1 Ne. 18:1). It makes little sense to the world, but it's the Lord's way of doing things—His effort to try us, to prove us, to test us, to refine us, one prompting and one act of obedience at a time.

I've read the Book of Mormon one hundred times. Don't be impressed. I have to read it and read it and read it to understand it because I'm dyslexic and I also have attention deficit disorder. Many times I've knelt and pled for the burning assurance that Moroni 10:4 promises. I've ached to know for certain that the book was true. I have friends for whom the witness was so strong that they've had smoke billowing out of their ears. Not me. I've never had that witness. Never. And yet one day I realized from the crown of my head to the tips of my toes that I know the Book of Mormon is true. It didn't come in a fiery revelation. It came in warm words and whispered truths and answers to my questions. It came slowly and after much effort, but it came.

Why does the Lord work this way? He's been around a while and knows what works best—and He knows us best. "Behold, ye are little children and ye cannot bear all things now" (D&C 50:40); "I will lead you along" (D&C 78:18).

Why does a baby learn in small stages? Because his body is following the design of his Creator. Watching a baby learn to walk is a powerful visual aid in understanding how the Lord deals with us. It gives us reason to be patient with ourselves and to forgive ourselves when we fall. It demonstrates why Jesus Christ atoned for not only our sins but also for our sorrows and our suffering too. He does not punish us to make us suffer any more than a father would push to the ground a baby who is just learning to walk. He stands ready and allows us to fall, to get back up, and to fall again until we are steady on our feet.

True YOU

Michelangelo, the most exalted of artists, said, "Every block of stone has a statue inside it and it is the task of the sculptor to discover it" (Frank Zollner, Thomas Poepper, and Christof Thoenes, *Michelangelo* [Vanity Press, 2010], 24). I believe that every human being has divinity encased within, and it is the task of its creator as well as itself to set it free. No human being is an end product; every being still breathing is a creation yet under creation.

Michelangelo knew he was an artist but he did not limit that artistic ability to one genre; he became a sculptor, painter, architect, and poet. You've heard the saying, "Jack of all trades, master of none." There are times to master one skill before moving on to the next. But you are a child of God, and you have the great gift of agency and the ability to achieve your dreams and fulfill your desires. You choose the person you want to be. You choose what you want to become. You choose your life, or life will choose for you. This step in the refining process involves your participation more than any other step.

Yes, our dreams are unlimited, but while the Lord works without limit, He also works within borders. Latter-day Saints know something of borders and boundaries. We talk of levels and doors and varying kingdoms. We have rules and commandments and covenants. We are a people bound by order, set by He who ordered the universe.

A Shape That Does Not Fit

Unfortunately, in our religious society we know something of judgments and limitations and trying to fit where we just don't fit. I spent most of my elementary school years growing up in Salt Lake City. I did not fit in my school class or my neighborhood, and I certainly did not fit in the one and only time I attended LDS Primary.

Primary was held on Wednesdays after school, and I was so excited to go. My friend Rebecca invited me. She didn't tell me I had to wear a dress, so I wore pants. It was no big deal to her, but it was to the Primary leader, a woman who reminded me of Barbie's mother in her bouffant hairdo and pink pencil skirt with tiny pink bows on her shiny shoes. I'd never seen a walking portrait of perfection, but to me, that's exactly what Sister So-and-So was—perfection.

I didn't belong, but, oh, how I ached to belong. When I walked in, I looked up and saw a giant painting of Jesus with sad eyes. There was something so real about that particular Jesus that my own eyes got a little teary. But soon I was lost in the chaos of kids running around the gym and teachers calling everyone into the chapel to sit still.

So there I was in pants while every other girl wore a Sunday dress. They smelled like Ivory soap. Because my mother smoked two packs of cigarettes a day, I reeked of tobacco. Is it any wonder that the woman in the pink suit took me out into the foyer beneath the watching eyes of Jesus?

"Honey," she said quietly, "this Primary is for Mormon children. I know where you live. I'd be happy to walk you home."

I wince remembering the pain of that revelation. I was out of place. I did not belong. I did not fit in. I wasn't good enough. Clean enough. Soft enough. Loved enough.

Jesus seemed to look down at me, sadder than ever.

I did not cry. Not in front of Jesus and certainly not in front of the lady in pink. I made it all the way down the sidewalk before I burst into tears.

Permission to Be Different

At the grocery store the bagger put my groceries in two different boxes. One box held canned goods, all the same shaped and sized cans. The other box held bulky items like potatoes and a long loaf of hard French bread that protruded far out over the edge. Both boxes had the word *mismo* stamped on the cardboard. *Mismo* in Spanish means "same." The boxes looked identical, brown and square. But they were not identical, and their contents were not identical.

Do you ever feel like you don't fit in—not even in church, where there is supposed to be a place for everyone? Welcome to my life.

I was not raised LDS, so even after all my years of Church membership, I still have a lot to learn. The other mothers in our ward knew about Scouting and all of the badges and ranks and requirements. It sounded like the devil's program to me.

I'm in need of more refinement than most LDS women. My children come from different ethnicities and cultures, so our family portrait doesn't homogenize. I am divorced in a society that values family above everything except God. I was raised on the streets and in foster care, so we have few meals when a stranger isn't included at our table. In our home you might hear the blessing on the food given in Danish or Spanish or Arabic. We listen to reggae, country, rap and David Archuleta. Some of us are small and some of us are not. There is no *mismo* in our family, but I hope there is unity.

I was blessed to have a special mentor who once taught me that I wasn't meant to fit in someone else's box.

When I was in second grade, my mother drove me to school one morning. She'd been out most of the night drinking and was hung over; as a result, she caused a bit of a scene as she let me out in front of all the students who were going into the school. I was fuming at her and red-faced with embarrassment. I was a volcano ready to blow when a sixth-grader—a big, burly boy—made a crude and cutting remark about my mother.

I dropped my books to the floor and charged that kid with my head down, like a bull with horns. I knocked the wind out of him, and he knocked me to the ground. In no time we were wrestling and fighting and rolling around in the school hallway, crashing into lockers and walls and each other. His nose was bleeding. My head was bleeding where I hit the heating vent. But I wasn't about to give up.

It seemed the entire school had gathered to watch.

Then a voice demanded, "Stop that now!"

It was a firm voice but not a bellowing one by any means. We didn't exactly stop, so the owner of the voice stepped in to separate us. She took an elbow to her own ribs and a kick or two to her shins before she got a firm hold on my neck. Because I was about her size, she grabbed me first. "I said, stop it!"

I looked into her red face and knew that I had disappointed her. I hated knowing that, because I loved Mrs. Okasaki.

She took both of us to the office, had the school nurse tend to our wounds, and then promptly expelled both of us. My mother came in, still hung over, and the fight threatened to erupt again— only this time it was my mother who pulled me off the boy.

I felt so embarrassed by my mother's inebriated state. I was angry with myself and so humiliated I couldn't even look Mrs. Okasaki in the eyes. She was the teacher who was kind, the one who taught me to read and who let me bring my pet garter snake for show-and-tell.

She was the one I never wanted to disappoint, and yet she was the one I'd let down.

That night I answered the door and there she was: Mrs. Okasaki with a book in her hand and my week's worth of homework in her purse. She'd gone to all the trouble to care about one student—a misfit, a misbehaved kid who didn't matter. And yet there she was acting like I mattered very much.

I did my best to tell her how I felt but she seemed to already know. She explained to me how she and her husband were some of the first Japanese faces to appear in their Salt Lake City neighborhood at a time when Japanese faces weren't welcome. She talked about how people misjudged them and misunderstood them. Then she told me stories about how they went out of their way to make friends out of enemies. She challenged me to do the same.

She taught me, "You came with your own shape. You came with your own experiences. You came to be you, not anybody else. If you try to fit into someone else's shape you're going to be uncomfortable and you will not have room to move or grow."

Before she left, she hugged me and said, "I know that your life is different from mine. That's okay. I give you permission to be who you are and who you can become."

I didn't think about her words as much as I remembered the feeling I got when I was in her arms.

Chieko Okasaki went on to become a great influence in my life and in the lives of my children. Those arms held me again and again and I will be forever grateful that she taught me that God did not create all of His children to look or act alike but that He does want us to be united. "Be one; and if ye are not one ye are not mine" (D&C 38:27). The Lord loves variety, not diversity. He loves unity, not division. *Unidos* is not *mismo*.

One in heart, mind, might, and spirit. By her brave and brilliant example, Chieko Okasaki set a precedent for me and for every other

Latter-day Saint woman who feels she doesn't fit a certain mold. Chieko was the first non-Caucasian to serve on a general board of The Church of Jesus Christ of Latter-day Saints. She was the first mission mother of the Japan Okinawa Mission. She traveled the world speaking for all of us who feel different.

At a fireside given not long before she fell fatally ill, Sister Okasaki spoke to this very point: "There are times we live cookie-cutter lives. For many, there comes a moment when those boundaries don't feel good or right anymore. That is the time when we need personal revelation from our Heavenly Father and our Heavenly Mother. They certainly don't expect us to lop off parts of ourselves or our lives to fit into someone else's shape."

Change

Changing shapes is difficult, even when it is a change for the better. Changing jobs is tough. I cried for a week when I was released from Cub Scouts, and I had detested that calling. When you move, when a friend moves, when you graduate, when a relationship ends, when a new opportunity opens, change is hard. But change is necessary if we are going to grow and become refined.

Gold cannot be what it is meant to be unless it goes through (note the word *through*) a change from liquid to solid. Only then can it be molded and shaped into what the Refiner has conceived.

My friend Stephanie grew up in Utah. When I met her she prided herself in staying "uninfected" by the Mormons. "They got my brother," she said, smiling, "but they'll never get me. It's not that what they teach is wrong, it's just that I don't need it."

Then Stephanie's only little girl grew began to grow up, and Stephanie decided it was time to teach Kenzie to pray.

"Repeat after me," she told her little girl. "Dear Heavenly Father."

Kenzie gave her mother a funny look but shrugged her tiny shoulders and said, "Dear Harry Potter."

That's when Stephanie knew it was time for a change.

The Mormons "got" her, and she was baptized.

And Stephanie lived happily ever after, right? You do the right thing and the right thing happens to you, right? Not in my experience. That's not how refinement works.

Shortly after her baptism, Stephanie's beloved father died. She was his only daughter, and he was her hero. I didn't think her broken heart would ever mend, but she took strength from a newborn testimony that she could be with him on the other side of the veil.

Then came the diagnosis that Stephanie had a brain tumor.

Seeing her stay true to her newfound faith through such trials strengthened all of those who know and love her. She's still strong. She's still valiant. She is refined.

If we are not changing, we are not living.

Until we take the shape that we are meant to be, until we are molded by the loving refinement of Christ, we are not complete.

What shape should be our goal? "Seest thou that ye are created after mine own image? Yea, even all men were created in the beginning after mine own image. Behold, this body, which ye now behold, is the body of my spirit; and man have I created after the body of my spirit; and even as I appear unto thee to be in the spirit will I appear unto my people in the flesh" (Ether 3:15–16).

God took the shape of man and was molded by the things He suffered so that we too might change to be more like Him.

CHAPTER EIGHT

A Final Separation

*"He is our Father and He loves us. Do not think that because
we are living on this earth away from Him and because
we can't see Him that He has forgotten us."*
—Boyd K. Packer

YOU'VE TAKEN SHAPE. YOU AND the rest of the world can see what you are becoming. You're far along in the refining process, but a final separation still has to occur.

Not everyone goes through this step. Some refiners, content with close enough, skip it altogether. Not yours. Not mine. Out of an unfathomable love for us, our Refiner continues to refine us until we are perfectly pure. I use the word *perfectly* on purpose. We might think of perfection as "an honest tithing" at the end of the year or a "perfect landing" in a gymnastics competition.

Jesus Himself called for our perfection when He said, "Be ye therefore perfect, even as your Father which is in heaven is perfect" (Matt. 5:48). That goal seems unattainable in my puny, mortal thinking. Every day I make mistakes. Some days I commit outright sin. Perfection in this life seems out of the question; refinement through the Atonement seems attainable, but not perfection. Yet Jesus would not have required it of us if it were not possible to attain.

The New Testament was first written in Greek; in that language, the term for *perfect* centered on the root *teleios*. It does not mean without flaw; it translates as "mature," "grown," or "having arrived at its end." It means "complete." This makes "perfect" sense when we consider what the sinless Son of God told the Pharisees not long before He was crucified: that on "the third day I shall be perfected" (Luke 13:32).

At the time Christ spoke these words, He had not atoned in the Garden or died on the cross or defeated death and received His resurrected body. As already established, God's pattern for getting things done is line upon line, precept upon percent. There is order and meaning and completeness.

Take heart! You and I are far from complete. This life is only a leg on our journey, so don't despair to know that even this final separation is really just a starting over. More heat. More additives. More filtering. More agitation. More waiting. More molding.

Translating *perfect* as "complete" gives us understanding that refinement rids us of our imperfections, those things that are not yet complete in us because they contain impurities. The Refiner's fire burns from us the impurities that keep us separated from God.

The Parable of the Potgut

In Utah, hunters call the Uinta ground squirrel by another name: potgut. These little rodent-like creatures are plentiful around Fish Lake. Their devotion to each other is commendable, and they are one of a handful of animals that mate for life. The summer I took my children to camp there the little animals were popping up all over the place. I barely missed hitting one on the road to our cabin; the next driver who came by wasn't so lucky.

The little animal lay dead in the center of the dirt road. The sight was a sad one, and it became utterly heartbreaking when the deceased's companion arrived to mourn. I had never seen such sorrow. The little animal made a shrill wailing sound. At first it sniffed its still partner and then did everything it could to nudge life back into the body. Next it rose up on its tiny hind legs and wailed louder than ever. After that it ran circles around and around its fallen partner. At last the potgut lay down with its head on the corpse and stayed put. My children went out to catch it and "cheer it up." I convinced them it was a bad idea.

The wailing continued for much of the night. The next morning I wailed too when I saw that both animals were unmoving in death, the second lying just as it had been the night before, its head pillowed on its fallen mate.

My daughter wept. "It died of a broken heart because they just couldn't stand to be apart."

She was right. At least a part of us dies when we become separated from those we love.

Spiritual Death

Physical death occurs when our spirits are separated from our bodies. Spiritual death is much more serious and occurs when we are separated from Heavenly Father. This happens because of Adam's transgression and because of our own transgressions, sins, and disobedience. Among the truths the prophet Samuel preached from the wall in Zarahemla was that "all mankind, by the fall of Adam being cut off from the presence of the Lord, are considered as dead, both as to things temporal and to things spiritual" (Hel. 14:16).

We know this separation does not last forever. The Resurrection of Jesus Christ redeems us from the jaws of death so that "all men come unto God; wherefore, they stand in the presence of him, to be judged of him according to the truth and holiness which is in him" (2 Ne. 2:10).

Note that we are not judged by the "truth and holiness" that is in *us* but the truth and holiness that is in the *Lord*. He is the only one worthy and qualified to judge, because it is His Atoning sacrifice that refines the impurities from our lives so we might qualify to return to the presence of Heavenly Father and defeat spiritual death.

Isn't this the best news you ever heard? Our refinement isn't for suffering or even polishing. It's not even just to make us pure. It is so that we can return to the presence of the God who gave us life in the first place, so that we can dwell with Him and become like Him.

Is it worth it? You tell me. Is anything worth separating us from God?

Nothing

I know a woman who had to make that very decision. Her husband started a business when they were newlyweds. When he was only twenty-seven years old he was called as a bishop, at the very same time he was beginning his doctoral studies, at the very same time she announced they were going to have a baby.

Three years later the doctorate was earned, the business was flourishing, another baby had been born, and he was still bishop. One night he went to bed with a business problem orbiting his mind. He dreamed a dream that gave him not only the answer to his problem but an idea for a new and exciting product. He woke up his wife to relate the dream, and she wrote it all down in her journal as he explained it.

At this point he decided to take on a business partner to ease his workload and free up time to spend with his family. That partner was a man who had served with him in the Church. My friend's husband confided in him the details of the dream. Together they worked on the new product.

The company grew steadily and brought more media attention and money than they imagined possible, all because of the product in development.

My friend's husband was released as bishop only to be called as stake president. Ten months later that partner sued my friend's husband, claiming that he had brought the product idea in the first place.

Immediately, the media picked up the story. My friend's husband's character was challenged. People gossiped. Friends took sides. Their finances were squeezed until no income at all was coming into their household. Legal fees mounted. They lost their home. My friend suffered a miscarriage five months into her third pregnancy. Her heart filled with bitterness toward the man who had once been her husband's friend and partner. She was called to testify in court, and the journal that contained details of her husband's dream was shown as evidence; it was mocked and determined to be something she had fabricated years afterward.

"For the first time in my life I hated someone," she said. "I truly hated that man."

This sad litigation went on for years. Her husband took a teaching job, and she worked as a secretary. They rented a basement apartment from a family in their neighborhood. Her husband continued to serve as stake president.

"At night my good husband would kneel in family prayer and ask the Lord to bless that man, to watch over his family as He watched over ours," she said. "He prayed that his former partner would have a change of heart and speak the truth. I couldn't even say amen to those prayers. Instead, I offered my own, asking God to bring vengeance down upon that man."

In the meantime, my friend's husband began a new business while still teaching school. His original product was developed and marketed—not by him or his partner, but by that partner's brother, who made millions of dollars.

"I knew exactly what had happened, and I knew the Lord knew," she told me. "How could He have allowed such a thing? My heart grew hard and bitter. I resented my husband for his continued prayers in behalf of our own family's enemies. Oh, I went on with my life. I loved my husband and supported him the best I could. I raised our children, I served dutifully in the Church, I worked until the new company was up and going."

The final judgment came down in favor of the partner, who was awarded the lion's share of the original company and 90 percent of the rights to the multimillion-dollar product.

"My hatred grew," my friend continued. "I wanted what was rightfully ours. Why had the Lord not stepped in to stop such a blatant injustice? My heart seemed to shrink into something hard and small. Then one day I was walking around the perimeter of the Provo Temple, where my husband and I now served as workers. The question came into my mind, *What is worth separating you from God?*

"*Nothing*, I thought, and I kept walking. Again, the question came, *What is worth separating you from God? Absolutely nothing.* The third time the question came: *What is worth separating you from God?*

"I nearly fell to my knees right then and there. That wicked man wasn't standing in my way—I was. It was my hatred and unforgiveness that was separating me from the kind of relationship I wanted and needed to have with Heavenly Father. I went home and knelt beside my bed. I prayed out loud, begging God to forgive me. I vowed then and there that no one and nothing was going to separate me from God because nothing was worth it."

Take Advantage of the Atonement

The Atonement is our hope. It is our way back. Life is tough. Because I know these things and have shared them in writing does not mean my problems have gone away. In fact, they've increased, but so has my ability to deal with them because now I understand what I didn't understand as well before: Refinement is a blessing—a glorious blessing at that. It means God hasn't given up on me. It means I have no right or reason to give up on myself.

I now understand the Atonement on a very personal level. "For all have sinned, and come short of the glory of God" (Rom. 3:23). Jesus values me enough to include me in His sacrifice. He atoned for my sins, my mistakes, my sorrows, and my shortcomings. He is my Savior because I need saving. There is no shame in that, no reason to hide because there is no place we can run where the Lord cannot find us. He knows what we think, how we feel, what we say in whispers, what we do behind closed doors. And still, He loves us and sees gold where others see only ugly ore.

To *not* take advantage of His Atonement would be a travesty. It would be selfish and just plain stupid. To attempt to abuse it would also be a travesty. "Remember the worth of souls is great in the sight of God; For, behold, the Lord your Redeemer suffered death in the flesh; wherefore he suffered the pain of all men, that all men might repent and come unto him" (D&C 18:10–11.)

How on earth do we take advantage of it so that every effort to refine us changes us for the better? You know the drill: The standard five or six Rs of repentance (recognition, remorse, restitution, reformation, resolution, etc.) do not seem adequate.

The Atonement of Jesus Christ is personal. To use it and use with an honest heart is what we have to do, no matter how difficult it may seem. If we've learned anything from studying the refinement process it is this: Strength comes from struggle. When you learn to see your struggles as opportunities to become stronger, better, wiser, then your thinking shifts from "I can't do this" to "I must do this."

Sacrifice

Have you ever felt prompted to give away something you want to keep? Have you ever held something back because you were afraid that if you were generous, you would be left wanting? The law of sacrifice is a vital part of the refining process. When we sacrifice the right thing for the right reason, we rid ourselves of the impurities of fear, greed, and selfishness. "I have decreed in my heart, saith the Lord, that I will prove you in all things, whether you will abide in my covenant, even unto death, that you may be found worthy" (D&C 98:14).

There have been times in my life when I've succeeded at keeping this law and other times when I've failed. Trust me—it truly is better to give than to receive. At Christmastime I'm blessed to participate in a program that allows children who have to give to children who have not. It requires sacrifice from the most innocent and honest. It means children have to earn money to spend on someone else. It's the best program I know of to feel the true spirit of the season.

This past year one boy, about eight, stood in front of me with his hand outstretched. "Here," he said, "these are my favorite dinosaurs. They're the only toys I've got."

Three small green dinosaurs lay in his palm. This little guy wasn't one of the kids on my list who was supposed to be giving; his name was on the list to receive. I didn't understand and thought there must have been a mix-up.

"They're my favorite," he said.

I could see that in how worn they were and how tender his expression was. I was tempted to fold his little fingers back around his dinosaurs and tell him to keep them—that we had plenty of toys without his having to sacrifice his "favorite" ones.

Something told me to accept them and I did. Instead of bursting into tears, the boy seemed relieved and grinned. "Merry Christmas," he said. "I hope the little kid who gets them will play with them as much as I did."

"I hope so too." Then I asked his grandmother, who'd brought him, to explain the switch.

"Oh, when he saw that he could sign up to receive or to give, he signed both lists."

I checked and, sure enough, his name was on both lists.

The grandmother smiled just as wide as her grandson, then with a wink, she whispered, "He told me that if he was going to get something, he'd better be willing to give something first."

It would be nice to give without the thought of receiving anything in return, but that's not the case with refinement. Besides, it's impossible to get "one up" on the Lord. As King Benjamin taught us, He's always ahead of us in His generosity and giving.

We are asking the Lord to make us into something more, something better. We sacrifice our sins and in return we are made pure. Sounds like a win-win agreement to me.

King Lamoni's father asked Aaron what he had to do to become refined—saved in the kingdom of God. "But Aaron said unto him: If thou desirest this thing, if thou wilt bow down before God, yea, if thou wilt repent of all thy sins, and will bow down before God, and call on his name in faith, believing that ye shall receive, then shalt thou receive the hope which thou desirest" (Alma 22:16).

Aaron is teaching him to repent of *all* of his sins.

What does the king teach us?

"The king did bow down before the Lord, upon his knees; yea, even he did prostrate himself upon the earth, and cried mightily, saying: O God, Aaron hath told me that there is a God; and if there is a God, and if thou art God, wilt thou make thyself known unto me, and I will give away all my sins to know thee" (Alma 22:17–18).

How many of our sins are we willing to give away to know God?

The Lamanite king made his sacrifice in sins, the widow made hers in coins, the little boy at Christmas made his in dinosaurs. What do we have to sacrifice to the Lord in order to know Him?

The Price of Readmission

To void the separation that exists between us and our Father in Heaven, we must take advantage of the Atonement. We must do all we can so that Christ can command the gates of heaven to swing wide open and allow us to enter. In the beginning of this book, we discussed the idea that the price of admission to enter this life was adversity. What's the price of readmission? It's a price we cannot pay, no matter what we offer. The good news, the great news, the better than best news is that the price of our readmission has been prepaid by the only One capable of paying it.

How do we use the Atonement for our ticket to readmission? It's something Amulek explained to Zeezrom: "The Lord surely should come to redeem his people, but that he should not come to redeem them in their sins, but to redeem them from their sins. And he hath power given unto him from the Father to redeem them from their sins because of repentance; therefore he hath sent his angels to declare the tidings of the conditions of repentance, which bringeth unto the power of the Redeemer, unto the salvation of their souls" (Hel. 5:10–11).

What are those conditions?

To believe in God. That He is. That He can. That He does.

To want to change—to feel the pressure in your heart, the softening that invites repentance.

To acknowledge that you've fallen and can't get up without God's mercy and strong arm.

To beg for help now, knowing that a final judgment awaits you and therefore you cannot wait or waste a moment thinking you'll repent later.

To extend forgiveness and mercy to ourselves and to others who fall and fall again.

To pray always and not allow yourself to become spiritually stagnant.

To be the voice that leads others to Christ, to be the hands that help carry others' burdens, to be the one who can be counted on to serve whenever and wherever you are called.

To realize there are no exceptions: No unclean thing can dwell with God.

To make the Atonement personal by crying out to Christ, who is the only one who can make us clean again. The ONLY ONE.

A New Meaning, a New Life, a New You

How does Christ do it? By refining us through fire until we are perfectly pure through His Atonement. Only then will the gates of heaven open for our readmission and the Master will rejoice, "Well done." (Doesn't that take on a new meaning worth smiling about when you think of the fire you've had to endure?)

Do not be discouraged. Be as Paul in the sewer dungeon when he said, "Rejoice in the Lord . . . and again I say, Rejoice" (Phil. 4:4).

Your past does not matter because it does not determine your future. You can launch a new life starting this very second. You can become a new creature in Christ. You can do it by taking advantage of the Atonement.

There is no other way.

CHAPTER NINE

Settlement

"*Remember the worth of souls is great in the sight of God.*"
—D&C 18:10

WE'VE COME TO THE STAGE of refinement when things finally pay off. Goldsmiths call it *settlement.* You hold in your hand an ounce of refined gold. What do you do with it? First, you find someone you trust to value it, because its worth depends entirely its purity. Not all gold is the same.

Gold is weighed in karats. A karat equals 1/24 part, so pure gold is 24-karat gold (all gold, no alloy). Other purities are measured the same way: 22-karat gold is twenty-two parts gold and two parts alloy; 12-karat gold contains twelve parts gold and twelve parts alloy. Alloy is a less costly metal made by combining two or more metallic elements, often copper or silver. This not only changes the constitution of the gold but even its color.

Just How Great

The world's economic markets determine the price of gold. God determines the price of a soul. The world measures our worth by how we appear, what we weigh, how much money we have accumulated, the size of house in which we live. The Lord values His children for reasons far different, for "the Lord seeth not as man seeth; for man looketh on the outward appearance, but the Lord looketh on the heart" (1 Sam. 16:7).

I had the honor of witnessing a baby elephant born in the wild. It was a miraculous sight as that mother strained and struggled to bring her baby into this world. Never for a second did I expect a giraffe to emerge from her womb. Or a gorilla. Or a parakeet. I expected exactly what I saw: a baby elephant, an adorable, miniature version of the mother. That mother weighed approximately eight thousand pounds while her baby tipped the scales at 230 pounds. Obviously, there was a lot of growing and changing to do, but from looking at the herd—which included a thirteen-foot-tall bull elephant—it was obvious that a baby elephant is divinely designed to do just that: grow to become like its parents.

For those of us who believe that we are literally spiritual children of God the Father, do we not realize the potential within us? Are we aware of who we really are in relationship to the very God who created the universe, who scattered the stars and aligned the planets?

The fire of refinement can be welcome only to those who remember and realize that they are literally spirit children of a God who knows and loves them. Otherwise, pain and adversity are just that—pain and adversity. Fire doesn't purify; it only burns.

You and I are not yet perfect. Far from it. That's okay, because we are on this earth at this time not to be refined, but to *become* refined. We are in a loving process of becoming who we are meant to be. Please don't be discouraged because you're not there yet; learn to recognize what's happening in your life. Pray for understanding. Pray for strength, for mercy, for an added measure of love—not just toward others, but also toward yourself.

The devil lies. Plain and simple. He will tell you that the pains of refinement are the pains of punishment by a God who doesn't know you, doesn't care about you, and perhaps doesn't exist at all. He will whisper in your ear when you are tired, discouraged, and distraught. He knows just what to say, because he too knows you. And you know him. Alma taught us all a test to determine between the devil and God: "Whatsoever is good cometh from God, and whatsoever is evil cometh from the devil" (Alma 5:40).

It's not always easy to detect what is good and what is evil, just as it is not always easy to detect 24-karat gold from 12-karat gold, or even from fool's gold.

Touchstone

In days of old a hard black stone, such as jasper or basalt, was used to test the purity of gold. The gold was rubbed across the touchstone, producing a mark on its surface. The goldsmith had a chart of graded colors to which he matched the mark. The more yellow it was the more pure it was; if it streaked red, he knew it contained large amounts of copper. This process, simple as it was, proved impressively accurate.

What are the touchstones that test our purity? Courage might be a touchstone for a soldier, patience for a teacher, endurance for a marathon runner. Howard W. Hunter said, "I suggest to you that the Lord has prepared a touchstone for you and me, an outward measurement of inward discipleship that marks our faithfulness and will survive the fires yet to come" ("The Lord's Touchstone," *Ensign*, October 1986).

We say we are Christians. We sing that we are children of God. We testify to the world that our religion is based on revelation and truth and that we have a living prophet. But what are our marks when our behavior is rubbed against the challenge of this single scripture: "Inasmuch as ye have done it unto one of the least of these my brethren, ye have done it unto me" (Matt. 25:40)?

The purity of our hearts and our lives, the measure of our conviction, is not in how many meetings we attend or how many callings we claim. It is in how obedient we are to the God we love, and it is in how we love others.

The standard by which all Christians are measured is Jesus Christ. That means none of us comes close. You know what? That's how it's supposed to be—for now and for a very, very long item to come. It doesn't mean we should not be working toward that goal—in fact, that is what refinement is all about—but we should never berate ourselves for falling short.

We don't know our value but we must know that God does. Sometimes all it takes for us to soar is to know that someone values us and believes in us. I used to work for a veterinarian, so I have a tremendous love for all animals. One day I was flower shopping with my children at an outside nursery. I went to pick up a tray of flowers when something snapped at my hand. A hawk was hiding between two shelves behind the tray of flowers I'd reached for. It looked injured and more scared than I was.

My children ran to tell one of the employees. I stayed and tried to keep my finger from being lopped off by the bird's snapping beak.

A man came running, wearing a fat leather glove in one hand and carrying a hand shovel in the other.

I pointed out the hawk and asked, "What can we do to help it?"

He shook his head and motioned for us to step back. Then he moved the flowers to expose the bird. It went berserk, flapping and screeching, its beak opening and closing like a vise. The man lifted his hand and I thought he was going to grab it to save it. Not the case. The man sheltered himself with the gloved hand while he raised the shovel high to bring it down on the hawk's head.

I grabbed his arm. "No! Please! Don't hurt it."

"I'm not going to hurt it, lady, I'm going to kill it."

"You can't do that!" my son screamed. "Every life is worth saving, even a mean one." The hawk ended up in our home until it was well enough to be released in the wild.

Mindful of You

Enoch was blessed to envision some of God's creations. He tried his best to describe the magnitude and majesty in saying,

"Were it possible that man could number the particles of the earth, yea, millions of earths like this, it would not be a beginning to the number of thy creations" (Moses 7:30).

You and I are the highest of all those creations. We are the mortals for which this earth was prepared. That means the mountains were formed for us, the seas were filled for us, and the plants, animals, flowers, and fishes are here for our benefit. Christ suffered "the pain of all men" (D&C 18:11) because to Him, the human soul is valuable beyond calculation.

The psalmist asked one of the most important questions ever asked: "What is man, that thou art mindful of him?" (Ps. 8:4).

Go for a moment to a garden to discover the answer:

"And he . . . kneeled down, and prayed,

"Saying, Father, if thou be willing, remove this cup from me: nevertheless not my will, but thine, be done.

"And there appeared an angel unto him from heaven, strengthening him.

"And being in an agony he prayed more earnestly: and his sweat was as it were great drops of blood falling down to the ground." (Luke 22:41–44)

It is beyond our ability to comprehend how Christ suffered, but it is not beyond our ability to believe that He suffered so that we might not have to suffer anything beyond the pain of the Refiner's fire. Repentance is all he requires when we sin:

Therefore I command you to repent . . . lest . . . your sufferings be sore—how sore you know not, how exquisite you know not, yea, how hard to bear you know not.

For behold, I, God, have suffered these things for all, that they might not suffer if they would repent;

But if they would not repent they must suffer even as I;

Which suffering caused myself, even God, the greatest of all, to tremble because of pain, and to bleed at every pore, and to suffer both body and spirit—and would that I might not drink the bitter cup, and shrink—

Nevertheless, glory be to the Father, and I partook and finished my preparations unto the children of men. (D&C 19:15–19)

Unto the children of men—that means you and me.

Christ explained His part. Peter explained our part: "Christ also suffered for us, leaving us an example, that ye should follow his steps" (1 Pet. 2:21). We do that by doing what He did—He loved. John declared, "God is love" (1 John 4:8). A study of Christ's life shows how He served, healed, taught, and exemplified the best of His Father. He did not love grudgingly or selfishly. He loved without thought of recompense.

We can say we love. We can proclaim our love. But only those who show their love truly love. Love requires action. Learning to love is a huge part of refinement. It requires us to serve, to be involved, to sacrifice, to give, to help and to heal, to teach and to listen. It requires us to forgive when we don't want to forgive and to give when we want to hold back. If you were going to take a class in spiritual refinement, love would be the teacher.

The Price of a Life

It's one thing to discuss the worth of a human soul, but how do you put a price on Christ's life? Thirty pieces of silver? What a mockery!

In real life, insurance companies must put a value on a life whenever there is a wrongful death claim against the company. In that case, the worth of a person is generally determined as the net present value of the potential earnings of the individual. If you're the widow of a rock star, your settlement for his death would surely be in the millions. If you're the widow of a janitor, your settlement would be far, far less.

A rabbi explained to me the horror of how Nazis determined the worth of a Jew. In life they had no inherent value. Only after death did a Jew have worth, because their corpses could be used for soap and chemicals, their skin for art canvasses, and their hair for pillows. I saw these things on display in the Holocaust museum in Jerusalem. Even the decision to gas rather than shoot Jews was made simply on the basis of financial factors. Cyclone B gas was a much cheaper— albeit more excruciating and agonizing—way to kill a Jew compared to the one cent it would have cost for a bullet.

To the Nazis, human worth was measured in utilitarian terms by what a person could produce, even in death. To God, your value is in who you are, not in what you do.

You are worth the price of God's Beloved Son, His perfect, pure, and completely refined Son. Next time you berate yourself or fail to see value in another human being, remember that you, my brother, my sister, are worth the price of Jesus Christ's life.

Seeing through Us

Some people are easy to love. Others are not. Perhaps that's because we can see only what's on the outside and assume what's on the inside, while "the Lord seeth not as man seeth . . . but the LORD looketh on the heart" (1 Sam. 16:7). To love ourselves is often the greatest challenge of all.

You've heard expressions like "He's a tough shell to crack" or "She's a rotten egg." There are reasons for those sayings. When I lived on a farm, one of my chores was to candle the chicken eggs. This was done in a darkened room with the egg held before a light. The light penetrates the shell and makes it possible to observe what is inside.

This is done to determine the condition of the shell and the potential inside that shell. I checked the air cell, the yolk, and the white of the egg. I looked carefully to see if there were any cracks in the shell, spots inside the egg, or development of germs. I also checked the shell for stains or blemishes. The shape of the egg was also considered.

Farm eggs or incubated eggs are candled to determine whether they are fertile and, if fertile, to check the growth and development of the embryo. This is an important and complex process. There is a certain way to hold the egg: in a slanting position, you grasp the egg by the small end and hold it between the thumb and tips of the first two fingers so it is secure when turned rapidly to the side. Turning the egg rapidly to the side then shifts the contents inside and allows you to view what is going on inside. The thicker the shell, as in brown eggs, the more difficult the egg is to candle. A spot can predict many things about an egg—some mean the egg is defective, others mean the egg is fertilized and will develop a chick. A candler has to be able to read those spots accurately.

In the United States, the US Department of Agriculture standards divide commercial eggs into three classes: AA, A, and B—in other words, best, better, and good. Grade AA eggs must be clean, intact, and normally shaped. The white must be clear and firm and the yolk free of blemishes. The air cell cannot measure more than an eighth of an inch. Grade A eggs permit a three-sixteenths of an inch air cell, and the white must be "reasonably firm." Grade B eggs allow some stains, watery whites, and dark yolks. Grade B eggs can't be sold to consumers but are used to make egg products.

In the candling process, rotten eggs are discarded—very carefully. A rotten egg that gets cracked open smells worse than a den of skunks, so it's important to remove it the same way you'd remove a ticking bomb.

Through this entire process, the only way to determine if an egg is Grade AA or rotten is to see what is on the inside.

Our Savior is the light that shines through us, and only He can see what is inside. Only He can judge the grade we receive: AA, A, or B. Best, better, or good. First, second, or third place. Gold, silver, or bronze metals. Celestial, terrestrial, or telestial.

Not Enough

It is not enough to know that we are children of God. It is not enough to have a testimony of Jesus Christ. It is not enough to recognize that our refinement is but a perfecting of our souls. It is not enough to know these things; we must do something about them. We must help each other, lift each other, and serve each other. We are not truly refined if we are not like Christ.

It was the rainy season in Africa, and along the border of Kenya and Tanzania the greenish-gold grass was growing tall and lush. It was astonishing how wild predators like cheetahs and lions could camouflage themselves so easily. One cheetah emerged right in front of our Jeep and seemed oblivious to our presence.

Our guide had taught us that if you want to be aware of what's really going on in a place like the African savanna, you have to study a predator. Focus on the eyes. See what the predator is seeing.

This particular cheetah was a full-grown male, a beautiful creature but terrifying at the same time. When I made the connection between that beast's eyes and its target, I realized with horror that one little zebra was in grave trouble. Luckily, that striped baby was sandwiched between two adult zebras who were his protectors. This gave me a little hope.

But then I saw the cheetah's attention shift. His eyes went to a water hole off to our left, at the bottom of a muddy escarpment. Halfway up was a small frantic antelope, stuck chest-deep in the mud. I felt sick when I saw that cheetah creep toward the trapped beast. I suppose it looked like an easier meal than a baby zebra sandwiched between two adults.

I felt ill. The others in the safari Jeep were excited. They wanted to watch a kill. I wanted to run away, but that would make an even easier target for the hungry cheetah.

We watched for what seemed forever as that little antelope struggled. I was sure it had worn itself out when the cheetah lowered its belly to the ground and crept forward until it was within striking distance.

"Run!" I whispered. At least I *thought* I whispered. Everyone in the Jeep turned to glare at me. When I looked back I saw that antelope do the impossible. One after another, its spindly legs pulled out of that mud until the animal was free. The cheetah made a rocket-fast run forward but stopped short of the liberated antelope. Even from a distance I could see its little sides heaving in and out as it attempted to catch its breath. The cheetah looked at the antelope, and the antelope looked straight back at the cheetah. They were seconds away from a deadly clash. But the cheetah did not move as the antelope loped to the top of the escarpment, falling a few times but rising again.

I expected it to disappear in its hard-won freedom, to join the rest of its herd grazing in the distance. Not so. Once the antelope reached the top of the climb, it did something that left me speechless. It stopped. It just stopped in the face of the cheetah that was continuing to make progress toward it.

That antelope could have taken off at full speed; it could have darted for its final safety. But it didn't. It stopped and made the most desperate call I've ever heard. I realized it was sounding a warning cry to the rest of its herd. It was letting its friends and family know that a hungry cheetah was in the vicinity.

Once that call was made, the rest of the herd picked up their heads and their feet and thundered off across the plain. Only then did that little antelope take off at full speed, safe from the cheetah.

I want you to think about that brave little antelope that instinctively stopped and put itself in the path of danger to cry a warning to the rest of its friends and family. To me, that is a portrait of bravery and refinement at its purest.

Love is what will set us apart and make us more precious than gold, which turns out to be nowhere near as valuable as a human soul—or as lasting. The Apostle Peter taught that "the trial of your faith [is] much more precious than of gold that perisheth" (1 Pet. 1:7).

Love is the touchstone of our refinement. Love, taught the Prophet Joseph Smith, "is one of the chief characteristics of Deity, and ought to be manifested by those who aspire to be the sons of God. A man filled with the love of God, is not content with blessing his family alone, but ranges through the whole world, anxious to bless the whole human race" (Joseph Fielding Smith, comp., *Teachings of the Prophet Joseph Smith* [Salt Lake City: Deseret Book Company, 1976], 174).

Love has been the goal all along.

The Reward of Refinement

"Come unto Christ, and be perfected in him, and deny yourselves of all ungodliness; . . . and love God with all your might, mind and strength, then is his grace sufficient for you, that by his grace ye may be perfect in Christ . . ." (Moro. 10:32–33).

To be perfected in Christ is to be complete. That is the end goal. In the meantime, we are on a wondrous journey. Every experience counts. Every lesson learned matters. Every person we encounter has value beyond human comprehension.

We now understand that refinement hurts. Change can be painful. But it's necessary if we are to become what we are capable of becoming.

I am a believer of Jesus Christ, of every word He spoke, of every act He performed, of every claim He made. I am a Christian. I accept full responsibility for this testimony, and I declare it with a heart bursting with love and burning to share it.

I describe myself as ordinary as dust—the same dust that God used to create Adam. The same dust that, under the right circumstances and pressure, forms diamonds. The same dust from which ore is made. The same from which gold is made. The same dust God used to fashion this world and countless other worlds. I am one of God's creations, and there is nothing ordinary about someone God created—especially when He used Himself as the perfect pattern and created us after His own image and likeness.

We, my precious, spiritual siblings, are children of our Father. Jesus Christ is our brother, the one Father appointed to save us when we fall, and we've all fallen. Some, like me, have fallen harder than others. I know what it is to be a sinner. I know what it is to feel the hand of the Savior grip mine and pull me from the pit. I promise you that if He will do it for me, He will do it for you, for He loves you with a love that is perfect in spite of the imperfections we bring to the altar. For there is no unblemished lamb save one, and one only. Our best will never be good enough when it stands alone, but it will always be sufficient when it is given with real intent and a contrite heart, coupled with the saving grace available to make up the difference.

I know the things presented in this book are truths that have worked in my life. I'm still in the beginning of the refining process; the heat is burning, and the impurities are only now rising. The gospel of Jesus Christ is a plan perfected. You and I are part of that plan. It would not be perfect without us, for we are God's children and it is His work and His glory to bring about our eternal salvation.

We are in good hands. We are in the loving care of the greatest Refiner of all; He who has passed through the fires is now the fire.

Because I know this, I can look forward to life and all that it brings. I can see my trials and accept them for what they are: opportunities to rid my life of impurities that would otherwise keep me from that readmission ticket that Christ purchased for us.

Life can be brutal. It's not meant to be fair, and it isn't. When the fire grows too hot and the acid burns too deep, we can call out to the Refiner and He will answer. Of this I promise.

At some point you and I will be able to see His image shining in our countenances, and that is when we'll know that the refining process is working and worth it all.

ABOUT THE AUTHOR

TONI SORENSON IS THE AUTHOR of a number of bestselling books for both the national and LDS markets. In 2006, her Covenant novel, *Redemption Road*, won the prestigious Association of Mormon Letters honor for novel of the year.

She is an avid student of the scriptures and wrote her novel *Master* after years of research on the life of the Savior. Her novel *Messiah* reflects a lifetime of study of the Book of Mormon and her testimony of the Savior's ministry on the American continent.

In her previous work, *Defined by Christ*, Toni teaches how we can see ourselves as the Savior sees us—and emphasizes the importance of defining our worth by the worth the Savior attaches to us.

Refined by Christ follows up by summarizing the powerful lessons she learned during her own refinement process and combines her personal experiences with scripture and the counsel of prophets and apostles.

The mother of six children, four sons and two daughters, Toni also has a beautiful granddaughter. She and her family live in Utah Valley and love to travel, play, and eat together.